ADVENTURES IN AWARENESS

Learning with the
Help of Horses

By

Barbara K. Rector

authorHOUSE™

1663 LIBERTY DRIVE, SUITE 200
BLOOMINGTON, INDIANA 47403
(800) 839-8640
WWW.AUTHORHOUSE.COM

First published by AuthorHouse 12/02/05

ISBN: 1-4208-5392-9 (sc)

Library of Congress Control Number: 2005905378

Printed in the United States of America
Bloomington, Indiana

This book is printed on acid-free paper.

Front Cover: Rollick Hearted Moses 2005

Artist John Rubino www.rubinosculpture.com born New York 1952 – Rubino has worked in metal sculpture since early childhood. Rollick Hearted Moses created from curved steel plate – recycled from underground oil tank.
Subject: Moses is a black and white Gypsy Horse gelding residing at Derby Pond Farm in Derby, Vermont where he, Susan and Carl Taylor co-facilitate psychotherapy and experiential learning.

To see more of Rubino's work please visit www.rubinosculture.com or contact him at john@rubionsculpture.com

Back Cover: Barbara and Jet Star, equine colleague at Strozzi Ranch where she is often guest faculty.
Photographer, Dave Harris of the United Kingdom at first annual Equine Guided Education Association Conference, Valley Ford, CA January 05 www.equineguidededucation.org

In Tucson, Arizona, in 1973, there was no context or conceptual reality available to support the experience of dying, time traveling to visit then husband and children during their day, while simultaneously enduring a life review process, and being with a VOICE FEEL – EMBRYONIC LIGHT urging me to go back. "Now is not your time my child, you must go back". A massive shift in my reality base continues to unfold thirty years later. The more I tell my truth to myself, the more information becomes available. How to synthesize, translate and share is my creative purpose and process. **ADVENTURES IN AWARENESS** (AIA) is the result.

Experiences teaching the in-service sessions for Sierra Tucson hospital staff during the early 90's became the seeds of **AIA**. Educating others in the methodology and processes   of the STIRRUP barn (Sierra Tucson's Integrated Riding Resource Program) provided valuable equine experiential learning for staff and me. Abundant opportunities to 'train' referent guest professionals from around the world served to hone and polish **AIA**. A bibliography of the significant authors and teachers who contributed ideas, theories, and concepts, which I have generalized to working with horses and people, is listed at the end of this handbook.

In the first section, I describe the **AIA** inner-active exercises, explain the concepts, the principles process, and illustrate with true stories possible outcomes. In the teacher's manual section, facility specifications and arrangements for safety assurance, staff development, both human and equine, are discussed. The final section of this Handbook works through a basic **AIA** five-day curriculum. In the Appendices are the bibliography, my vitae, and information on further study with the **Adventures In Awareness Internship Program** (<u>www.adventuresinawareness. net</u> professional facilitator training workshops, as well as student internship opportunities.

TABLE OF CONTENTS

DEDICATION

For my Mom, Kathleen Rector, without whom there would be no **ADVENTURES IN AWARENESS™ (AIA),** and precious daughter, Kelly, Kathleen Rector Morken.   Both these women gracefully support with actions, words, deeds, and faith my enthusiasm for equine facilitated experiential learning process work. Kelly's horse, Vargas, helped invent **AIA**. He continues to engage, challenge, and love me.

Thank you Mom, Kelly and Vargas.

2004/05 UPDATE

Kathleen Spriggs-Wager Rector Dayton Jones Wyckoff (November, 1917) - yes, that's right, four husbands, all remarkable men in their own right, who with exception of my friend "acquired step-dad" Bill Wyckoff preceded Mom in their adventures to the other side of this physical veil. - Mom left the evening of April 1, 2004 at 7:40 pm.

The **Adventures In Awareness** website: www. adventuresinsawareness.net has a story in the archives section about Mom and Vargas, titled NOT DONE YET, that illustrates the splendid essence of both these amazing individuals. Vargas left for the other side, September 17, 2002. Their energetic heart presence continues to support and influence my work.

ACKNOWLEDGMENTS

My gratitude to my brother, Walt Rector, and my sister, Susan Semmens is boundless. Their faith, prayers, and unconditional love sustain and enrich my life. To my son, Bob Morken, his lovely wife, Yvonne, and their amazing daughters, Annika, Maya, and Ronja – I feel richly blessed with your generous hospitality, love, and fun times.

And thank you precious friends who believe in me even as I sometimes falter in my vision, mission, and purpose: treasured Bazy Takersley, Nancy McGibbon, Ann Alden, Mary Heldenbrand, Meira Yaer, Rebecca Bombet, Margaret Carroll, Jack Staudcher, Maureen Vidrine, Liz Baker, Molly DePrekel, Laura Brinkerhoff, Boo McDaniel, Maureen Fredrickson MacNamara, Franklin Levinson, Stephanie LaFarge, Shelly and Allen McColm, Valerie Sweeten, and Deb and Jim Harper. Your cheerleading combined with quality mentoring continues to sustain me.

Thanks, Mers, for making this book a reality!

Over the years, several amazing and talented students have participated in **AIA** as student interns with energy, brilliance, and hard work. They ask grand mystery questions, and contribute rich resourceful equine interactive exercises.

My thanks and admiration to Kelly, Julie, Kristin, Leif, Stephanie, Laura, Darren, Petra, Matt, Devon, Sara, Laura C, and Craig. You were present during many of the stories illustrating this handbook. Thank you for teaching me.

Thank you **AIA** herd: Vargas, Rama, Voo Doo Dream, Friar Tuck, Sea Sea Ryder, and AM Village Maypol (Maple), and AM Lizzie and River Ripple Babe both now deceased.

Missy Bear, I'm grateful for your continued personal companionship. Buttercup and Mitzi – staying alive, mousing and snaking. Thanks!

In addition, thank you **AIA** session, TASTE OF **AIA,** and **AIA**/EEL Institute participants. What a grand **ADVENTURE IN AWARENESS!**

Update: 2004/05

The **AIA**/EEL Institute has morphed into the **Adventures In Awareness** Internship Program (**AIA** IP), a 14 day curriculum of intensive study in theory, principles, and practice of equine facilitated experiential learning process work (defined as **Adventures In Awareness (AIA)**), interfaced with a three category enrichment menu of choices for intentional depth study and practice in the field of equine guided education and equine facilitated mental health. Specifics of **AIA** IP found on website: <u>**www.adventuresinsawareness. net**</u>

ADVENTURES IN AWARENESS LEARNING WITH THE HELP OF HORSES

PREFACE

In April of 1993, as I drove to work at Sierra Tucson Hospital, Inc. - a long commute around the mountain to Catalina, now that I lived at Morningstar in Tucson, Arizona, helping my mom deal with her husband's serious terminal illness - I pulled the car to the side of the road to write the following purpose statement for **ADVENTURES IN AWARENESS.** It was several minutes before I realized that there was a highway patrol officer tapping my car window to see if I was okay.

Recently, I had completed an enormous training project teaching each employee at the hospital what I now call **ADVENTURES IN AWARENESS (AIA).** As a result of sharing equine facilitated experiential learning process work with several hundred staff members of vastly different educational backgrounds - medical director, physicians, nurses, administrators, psychologists, and counselors, to dishwashers, housekeeping, and maintenance - **AIA** was born.

That day I wrote:

The purpose of **ADVENTURES IN AWARENESS (AIA)** is to develop awareness and expand consciousness while enhancing an individual's self-confidence through work with horses. Horses are compassionate teachers of basic life skills. During an **AIA** session, participants learn principles of responsibility, relationships, and communication, including inter-species communication. **AIA**'s uniquely designed interactive exercises with horses provide an interesting and fun process for awakening self empowerment, while promoting team building, and interpersonal relationship skills.

A growing body of clinical evidence suggests that people experiencing authentic empowerment through work with animals, especially large animals such as the horse, make healthy behavior choices; thus, contributing to reduced societal violence.

INTRODUCTION

The **ADVENTURES IN AWARENESS (AIA)** *process* promotes working with horses as an experiential (learn by doing) educational opportunity. Horses behaviorally mirror our interpersonal relationship dynamic. Acute observation, mindfulness practice, of these inner-active **gestalts** by facilitator(s), group members, and safety support staff produces remarkably accurate pictures of psyche's inner process. The word, **gestalt**, as defined by Webster's New Collegiate Dictionary is: "a structure, configuration, or pattern of physical phenomena so integrated as to constitute a functional unit with properties not derivable from its parts in summation".

As in the practice of dream work, this noticing of expressed observations *with attention and intention* through the feedback process (discussed in the round pen reasoning chapter) and linked to current life situation produces self-directed insights. "When the student is ready, the teacher (teaching) appears."

Participants explore what horses can teach humans about life skills. **AIA's** specifically designed interactive exercises focus on the development of relationship skills, while providing opportunities to practice interpersonal communication, including inter-species communication.

The intention of **AIA** is to develop personal reflective skills grounded in self-responsibility, while expanding awareness to become more fully conscious of internal thoughts that contribute to one's experience of reality. Expanded consciousness is associated with developing empowerment. Authentically empowered individuals make healthy behavior choices, living comfortably in peace and support of one another and our planet.

The purpose of this handbook is to set forth the basic principles of equine facilitated experiential learning (EFEL), as developed, practiced, and taught by myself, the originator of **ADVENTURES IN AWARENESS (AIA)**. The AIA process is a template, giving structure and form, for the teaching and practice of equine facilitated experiential learning process work, the term coined to describe equine facilitated experiential learning – **EFEL**. It is generally the professional educator (professional horse person) who actually teaches **EFEL**. Often, **AIA** is the treatment approach utilized by the licensed/credentialed mental health professional in the practice of equine facilitated psychotherapy (**EFP**).

Frequently people ask me how I came to this work. Where did I get the notion that animals communicate with humans? How can I believe that certain animals, like certain human beings, and particular places in Nature, are highly evolved spiritual guides offering wisdom and counsel in creating increasingly peaceful, mutually supportive, interdependent relationships nurturing harmony and balance (mentally, emotionally, physically, and spiritually) with a reality of inclusive abundance?

The truth is I have always lived in a world where animals and nature communicate. This reality went underground as I matured in the environment of collective culture, media managed childcare practices, and limitations of group mind school curriculums. Phrases such as "you are such an imaginative child, learn to live in the real world, live up to your potential, stop daydreaming and get with the program," peppered my youth and young adult life. And I continued to sit on rocks and become rock, lean into a tree to be tree.

In May of 1973, a near death experience (**NDE**) provided the impetus to co-found Therapeutic Riding of Tucson, Inc. (TROT), with my best friend, Nancy McGibbon and the mentoring support help of our friend, Bazy Tankersley. The integration of this NDE is something I am still living. Then, in the activity of being a corporate wife, mother of two bright, precocious children, and an active junior leaguer establishing a beneficial community health and educational service (TROT), this intense experience burrowed deep within my psyche.

In Tucson, Arizona, in 1973, there was no context or conceptual reality available to support the experience of dying, time traveling to visit then husband and children during their day, while simultaneously enduring a life review process, and being with a VOICE FEEL – EMBRYONIC LIGHT urging me to go back. "Now is not your time my child, you must go back". A massive shift in my reality base continues to unfold thirty years later. The more I tell my truth to myself, the more information becomes available. How to synthesize, translate and share is my creative purpose and process. **ADVENTURES IN AWARENESS (AIA)** is the result.

Experiences teaching the in-service sessions for Sierra Tucson hospital staff during the early 90's became the seeds of **AIA**. Educating others in the methodology and processes of the STIRRUP barn (Sierra Tucson's Integrated Riding Resource Program) provided valuable equine experiential learning for staff and me. Abundant opportunities to 'train' referent guest professionals from around the world served to hone and polish **AIA**. A bibliography of the significant authors and teachers who contributed ideas, theories, and concepts, which I have generalized to working with horses and people, is listed at the end of this handbook.

The evolution of this work and its theory base is liberally illustrated with personal stories of the horses whose identities have not been disguised. In the case of the people involved, their names have been changed in order to preserve the privacy pledged to each person in an **AIA** session.

People often ask about the significance or importance of consciousness. How does awareness contribute to knowledge of personal beliefs? And what is the effect on an individual's quality of life? The following story from the early days of STIRRUP illustrates possibilities. For me the story offers a description of both the **AIA** process and life lived in relationship.

At the hospital in Catalina, Arizona, the medical director was touring with a visiting dignitary, a nationally known and respected psychiatrist famous for his research protocols.

> They visited the barn, and this distinguished guest challenged me to explain equine facilitated psychotherapy in three sentences or less. The three of us were propped up against the arena fence observing the therapy horses turned out as a herd. We had been observing the antics of one particular bay horse in his efforts to keep the flirtatious red mare from enjoying the attentions of the other geldings.
>
> "Well, which one of these horses are you feeling drawn to and why?" I asked.

"Oh, that handsome bay! He's so charismatic and vibrant! While he's not having much luck keeping the mare away from the other guys, he's surely willing to prance and dance for her attention.

"In fact, now that I really notice him, he doesn't seem really confident off by himself. He wants that mare to give her attention and affections only to him."

"And how much have you told me about yourself?" I inquired of him.

After a moment of blank stare and a pregnant pause, his face suffused with emotion and his eyes became moist, "Why, I've told you more about me just now than I've told my analyst."

NOTE: This story is about people who **work** in the mental health field. It illustrates the significance of mental health professionals developing peer-counseling relationships for the purpose of continuing to work through to conscious awareness their own internal material. A helping professional (this includes credentialed instructors and educators) may only give to another that which they already possess. In working with people and their wide variety of life situations, issues and experiences, it is particularly important for the EFEL educator and EFP practitioner to continue to work on achieving personal clarity.

Basic Procedures

The **AIA** process promotes the **teaching of EFEL** and the **practice of EFP** through an interdisciplinary team approach.

For EFEL, this triad-teaching unit consists of the horse, the horse professional or credentialed instructor, and the professional educator. In the practice of EFP, the licensed health professional joins the horse professional and the horse to form the treatment team.

The educator or health professional has a trust agreement and an ethical responsibility to be fully attentive and present for the individual or group participants during an **AIA** session. Our colleague, the horse, subject to its instinctual nature (fight, flight, freeze or faint), also requires full attention and support. In the **AIA** process, while the staff is often cross-trained with appropriate credential and license, one person takes the horse safety support role, and one person takes the facilitator role (educator or health professional). It is interesting to note that frequently this role shifts. To a disembodied observer one might observe the identified educator to be the horse person and vice versa.

An **AIA** precept: **"You don't do this work alone."**

For group sessions, often the case in **AIA**-based programs, the additional staff required are trained, seasoned horse people who function as the safety support person for the horse. **By design, there are fewer horses than participants.** Just as we share parents, teachers, siblings, bosses, friends, we share **AIA** horses. Even the termed "one-on-one" sessions share the horse with the educator/health professional, horse professional, and participant.

Ideal group size depends on the intention and focus of the **AIA** session. I have worked with trained **AIA** co-facilitators to share an overview of **AIA** for 80 to 120 people. Eight to nine horses worked for the daylong session each with its personal safety support person and a lunch break with additional processing time for both horses and people.

For the **AIA** five-day curriculum, and introductory **AIA** sessions focused on specific topics, leadership, staff development, eco-environmental psychology, living in relationship, family group dynamics, interspecies communication, etc—ideal group size is six to eight. For introductory **AIA** sessions, the first three hours of **AIA**'s curriculum, 12 to 15 may be a comfortable number. Be mindful the size swells with inclusion of a trained equine safety support advocate for each horse. This size works well for older youth and their accompanying adult staff.

In the first section, I describe the **AIA** inner-active exercises, explain the concepts, the principles process, and illustrate with true stories possible outcomes. In the teacher's manual section, facility specifications and arrangements for safety assurance, staff development, both human and equine, are discussed. The final section of this Handbook works through a basic **AIA** five-day curriculum. In the Appendices are the bibliography, my vitae, and information on further study with the **Adventures In Awareness Internship Program™ (www.adventuresinawareness. net)** professional facilitator training workshops, as well as student internship opportunities.

THE HUMAN AIA STAFF

The concept of mindfulness of self suggests that the facilitator, the horse professional, and the safety support staffs are well trained and experienced in the AIA process. They engage in equine facilitated experiential learning process work for themselves with each other during regular in-service and staff development training sessions.

The educator takes classes and course work to increase knowledge and skill base, belongs to a regular meeting study group or book club, and participates in several yearly conferences, continuing education workshops and seminars. Ideally, they also take riding lessons. Perhaps they own their own horse, or share with another the lease of one with whom they may continue to learn under professional supervision.

The AIA horse professional actively trains and schools project horse(s), and teaches students who may compete in their particular specialty discipline. They attend clinics and conferences at least twice a year, while also working with a riding coach.

The health professional is in a peer support group, has a formal supervision arrangement with an advanced clinician, attends conferences and continuing education workshops and seminars, and takes riding lessons. **All AIA staff members are active participants in their own inward journey process.** Learning more about our interior process, psyche's inner workings, is key to our emerging sense of how the world works, and our personal responsibility for contributing to the safety of the group.

THE AIA HORSE STAFF

The qualified **AIA** horse, suitable for a trial period (90 days) in **AIA** equine facilitated experiential learning process work is kind, comfortable with groups of people working around him/her, stands quietly while tied, is bright of mind, and full of energy, with three quality symmetrical gaits. Such a horse is comfortable with a full developmental vaulting team of trained horse handler (either leading or ground driving), two side walkers, and mounted gymnastic work.

Ideally, the horse's back is well muscled, and strengthened through regular schooling of basic dressage figures at walk, trot, and canter by an educated rider.

Sensible and willing on the trail, alone or in company, the suitable candidate has mastered thinking for self while joining with humans in a mutually enriching and beneficial relationship. Said horse is not shut down or turned off by work. Has a strong sense of self and can handle life in a herd of both mares and geldings. The exceptional horse enjoys the round pen reasoning exercises and is open to developing bridle less riding skills. It is helpful if the horse is okay with either English or Western tack, especially the pad and surcingle. Generally, only snaffle bits are used. People new to mounted work will have reins attached by clips to the halter underneath the headstall (side pull style).

Basic good health is required. The **AIA** barn manager works with the owner on individual eating plans and necessary supplements. It is understood that most horses have unique conformation characteristics that may result in "serviceable soundness" situations.

AIA utilizes the services of a skilled veterinarian, cross-trained and/ or in collaboration with a professional acupuncture practitioner, chiropractor, equine masseuse, and equine dentist. The farrier is trained in orthopedic techniques utilizing the forge, (hot or cold shoeing), and works in collaboration with the vet. Regular trims for the barefoot horse are essential. It is an **AIA** policy to avoid dependence on pain killer medications; it is used sparingly on occasion for the older arthritic horses. **AIA** prefers to utilize the vast array of herbal solutions, chondroitin sulfate, glucosamine, MSM products to keep aging bodies comfortable.

Generally, the **AIA** herd contains both mares and geldings, (often mules, donkeys, minis horses and/or ponies as well) of all different ages. It is helpful for **AIA** groups to have experience of "new in the learning curve," as well as "wisdom filled school teacher," with a wide variety in between.

It is an **AIA** precept that certain individual horses, like particular people, have attained such expanded consciousness that they have volunteered as teachers to facilitate our developing awareness.

BASIC PRINCIPLES OF AIA

Now let us discuss the basis **AIA** principles, as they are presented in the **AIA Internship Program** professional facilitator training workshops. These principles are reviewed the first evening.

Think of the six basic concepts required of dressage riders while schooling their horses: Rhythm, Suppleness, Contact, Straightness, Schwung, and Collection.

1. **Rhythm:** a regular, cadenced flow to the work. This is true of the individual participants, as well as the collective group energy. Awareness of feelings within each participant is part of the "being responsible for self" and thus contributing to the safety of the group. The facilitator's role is one of alert monitoring, being mindful of self and of the surrounding group energy, including the horse.

For successful and safe rhythm and flow, an atmosphere of safety is vital. In an environmental ambience of "it's not possible to make a mistake," the notion of sharing uncomfortable feelings out loud first with the horse and then the group, unfolds naturally with practice and support.

This first principle contains elements of the unique **AIA** verbal safety agreement made by all present at the beginning of each session. The statement is, **"My name is . . . . and I agree to be responsible for myself today, and thus, contribute to the safety of the group."** This is a huge declaration. An individual fully aware of personal responsibility at all levels for physical, mental, emotional, and spiritual safety and in continuous mindful practice of such intentional living probably does not need an **AIA** session. For the rest of us, group support in consciousness assists with our practice of such a truth. Consciousness and the role it plays in creating the reality we experience is explored by Stan Grof, M.D. in his book, *The Holotropic Mind.*

Notice with care, how individuals choose to say the safety agreement. Frequently, well trained by our culture, they unconsciously state willingness to assume responsibility for the entire group's safety. An individual can only **contribute** to the safety of the whole group. The one person an individual is capable of being responsible for is self. Thoroughly discuss what it may mean to each participant to be responsible for self around large animals, whose behavior is unknown or not familiar. Be clear as to how to call a "time-out" if safety is an issue or directions are not clear. It is okay to ask for help, and express feelings of being uncomfortable or not safe—physically, mentally, emotionally, or spiritually. **AIA views this self-monitoring consciousness practice as a major metaphor for mastery of life skills on life's terms.**

Integrity of group process is honored with contracts for not speaking about individuals or personal incidences outside the group. It is okay to speak of the situations and tell horse stories, but it is imperative that names of people are withheld. The agreement to hold confidential the names and activities of other participants frees the group to fully express personal insights, perceptions, and processing.

The **AIA** rule of "it is not possible to make a mistake" is reviewed. *Keep self safe. You cannot be wrong.* An attractive notion—not being wrong.

However, life spent in this thought form requires relinquishing being right. The resulting discovery of **the freedom to be authentic is precious.** Unconditional acceptance brings forth creative expression.

INSIGHT DEVELOPMENT

2. **Suppleness:** the ability to bend both laterally and longitudinally; moving off in response to the leg with lightness and energy.

Equine facilitated experiential learning is a process. Individual insights are self-developed through relationship, and interaction with other people, horses, places, and situations.

Ideally, the group as a whole enters the TAO. Akin to Maslow's concept of peak experiences, the TAO is a non-ordinary state of consciousness sensed as an energetic flow weaving together horses, participants, and AIA staff in an effortless flow. Direct experience of the TAO includes a quality of timelessness, extraordinary sense perceptions, and numinous feelings of unity.

It is important for the facilitator(s), the educator and/or the mental health professional, and the horse professional (credentialed instructor), to monitor this flow of energy with the horses, with the participants, and with themselves. Developing skills in mindful monitoring of this energetic flow of equine facilitated experiential learning process work while simultaneously teaching FEEL/or practicing EFP is the intent and focus of the **Adventures In Awareness Internship Program (AIA IP™)** facilitator training workshops.

AIA's equine facilitated experiential learning process promotes insight development through interactions with the horses and other group members. Knowledge of one's relationship to self is developed through reflection, insight processing, feeling feelings fully, and feedback from both the group and the horses, thus developing and practicing interpersonal communication skills. Dr. James J. Lynch in his book, *A Cry Unheard, New Insights into the Medical Consequences of Loneliness,* has linked the failure to develop comfort with communication (human to human dialogue) with physiological changes (heightened blood pressure and adrenalin levels – activation of the fear/flight response) in the human body that lead to premature death through early heart disease and adult onset diabetes.

One of the primary purposes of **AIA** is to explore the relationship with a power greater than ones self, the God of one's personal understanding. **AIA** sessions do not seek to change or promote a particular belief in The Divine Organizing Principle. Rather, **AIA** sessions offer the opportunity to investigate one's personal beliefs, thoughts, ideas, and feelings about a power greater than self. **A precept of AIA is the notion that relationship with one's Higher Power is primary to developing relationship with self, and only then is it possible to develop relationship with another.**

During **AIA** sessions, participants learn to investigate what it is they do believe. The interactive exercises with the horses and with each other offer opportunities to examine what conceptual framework of reality shapes their experiences of life. I agree with Stan Grof when he says most people are unaware that they live in a "hamburger stand, fast food, media managed collective reality," a made up story of how the world works that people unconsciously accept as true. Just as years ago, prior to actual investigation by a few brave souls, people lived with the limits of a flat world.

One of the learning goals in **AIA** is to develop familiarity with the flow of energy as expressed through the horse's behavior. An initial inner-active and interactive exercise is to mindfully heart scan the herd as they romp and play together at the start of work. This herd activity directly mirrors (reflects back to the observing group) a precise picture of the observing human group's interactive dynamic.

Jung's archetypes, universal symbols common to all cultures such as "Mom", "Child", etc., are present in the herd and present in the group. After a period of time, ask the observing participants to pick out the herd leader; the administrative assistant or second in command; the loner or lost child; the behavioral acting out troublemaker; the okay with just going along with the group; the bold, wants you to think he/she is the leader, etc. Ask the participants why they made that particular choice. Listen closely to the answers, the rational of choice. Notice carefully what the perceiver perceived.

Another **AIA** principle may be stated, **"What I see in you is also in me"**. More about the action of this principle is discussed in the section on the mechanisms of projections, transference, and counter-transference. For a specific example of the concept of projection at work, re-read the story of early days at Sierra Tucson, when the visiting psychiatrist asked me to explain EFP.

All people present are full participants in an AIA session. There are no identified experts, helpers, students, teachers; all are involved as full participants. Yes, the group is facilitated, and the horse professional, and safety support people for the horses are identified, and *ALL are participants.* The horse makes no distinction between the identified professional facilitator and the learning participant.

A precept contained in this principle of suppleness, bending laterally and longitudinally, is the notion that in order to effectively guide, teach, or give, one must first have journeyed, learned, or acquired for self with consciousness.

CONNECTION OF MIND, BODY & SPIRIT

3. **Contact.** Connection between horse and rider established in mounted work through a gentle chewing feeling with rider's fingers on the reins, and a responsiveness to shifts in seat (body weight) and pressure from the legs. The horse is on the aids, in front of the rider, a feeling of reading the rider's mind (front brain). Conscious connection of mind/body/spirit is essential.

Each time we fall out of alignment we are subject to an addictive (distorted and/or dysfunctional) thought, behavior, attitude, and or process. When we are conscious of utilizing our powerful mind in service to our compassionate heart, we are attuned to the **energy** of universal wisdom and divine intelligence. The power of conscious choice and right use of will is accessed. Such congruency of emotions with mind/body/spirit is to experience peace in the present – NOW.

Gary Schwartz, PhD, and Linda Russek, PhD, who direct the Human Energy Systems Laboratory at the University of Arizona, have shown that the electrical impulses generated by one person's heart (measured by EKG) can affect the electrical impulses in the brain of another person (measured by EEG) sitting a few feet away. (Schwartz and Russek, *The Living Energy Universe* (Hampton Roads, 1999).

Both Paul Belik, a dressage rider and trainer, and John Lyons, a round pen teacher-trainer speak of the horse's capacity to tune into 'pictures' from the rider's front brain. Many of us in schooling and or pleasure riding relationships with a particular horse recognize the experience of the horse seeming to read our mind.

An AIA principle is that the horse is reading the energy of the primary handler, and reflecting with their behavior an interior 'gestalt' view of this individual' internal process. We will discuss this further as we explore the AIA interactive exercises in subsequent chapters.

Larry Dossy, M.D. discusses further information on Energy and its influence on our lives in his book, *Reinventing Medicine.* The well-researched conceptual framework presented by Dr. Dossy offers the context of Three Eras of Medicine. EFEL and EFP fit nicely into his Third Era of shared mind.

Liana Rubenfield discusses the principles of energy and offers further perspective in her book, *The Rubenfield Synergy Method*; a system of learning touch. A symphony conductor before becoming a psychotherapist, she has synthesized universal harmonics with sensorial principles of movement and touch. These two theory bases, when generalized to wellness work with horses, produce a solid conceptual framework for equine facilitated experiential learning process work.

Carolyn Myss, PhD, in her book, *Spiritual Anatomy,* discusses the disease processes in our bodies resulting from energetic blocks to awareness created unconsciously through distortions in our thinking. Trained as a theologian, Dr. Myss sought universal truth in the far eastern thought system of energy chakras. In her teaching, she ties the chakras to the seven sacraments of Christianity as well as to the seven branches of the Judaic Tree of Life. Further discussion of the chakras and their significant connection to our work is focal point of book number two, *AIA's JOURNEY RIDE.*

Andrew Weil, MD, Director of Integrated Medicine at the University of Arizona, speaks often of the connection between expanded awareness and developing consciousness and the experience of spontaneous healing – miracles. There is compelling evidence for us, as individuals, to mindfully journey inward and explore the final frontier of our own psyche, while simultaneously; consciously interdependent, practicing right use of will with compassion for others, and, thus, ourselves.

4. **Straightness:** refers to the path of travel; the horse's body remains straight while traveling on a circle or in a straight line.

As metaphor for principles of the AIA process, straightness refers to the integrity of the horse. A horse is honest. Even if dishonest, a horse is experienced as honestly dishonest. These are generally man-made situations. **Basic to AIA is the notion that the** horse's behavior reflects the inner process (thoughts, feelings, emotions, attitudes) of the primary person interacting with the horse at any given moment. The horse's behavior energetically mirrors that of the handler.

Simultaneously it is important to remember that a horse is always a horse first; ingestive behavior (eating) prevails; a horse awakens each day subject to its instinctual prey nature - the thought form of being someone's breakfast - flight or fight, freeze or faint.

HOLDING THE PICTURE IN YOUR MIND

Students at Prescott College in Prescott, Arizona, who seek to learn about Animal Assisted Therapy (AAT), take a course entitled, "Therapeutic Work with Horses and Experiential Learning Principles Through the Lens of **ADVENTURES IN AWARENESS**". This course introduces the student to an effective model for assisting youth at risk, people in changing circumstance, and/or those wrestling with grief or loss, to the interactive experience of horses as compassionate teachers of basic life skills.

The **AIA** process works with horse as a reflective mirror of our interpersonal relationship dynamic, and provides an interesting wakening to our personal capacity for empowerment. The specially designed interactive exercises develop communication (including inter-species), as well as intuitive and self-reflective skills that increase the quality and precision of a student's capacity to attend effectively to themselves and others. Clinical evidence suggests that authentically empowered individuals make healthy behavior choices, thus, reducing societal violence.

The course includes as an optional text, His Holiness, The Dalai Lama's **Ethics for the New Millennium**. The essential message of this book is the incredible significance of the thoughts we think in creating and bringing to manifestation our experience of reality. The ethics for this next portion of our evolutionary journey is to become intensely aware moment-by-moment of the thoughts we think. Our task is to develop mindfulness, as these thoughts are literally prayers sent out into our "Field of Infinite Possibilities," developing into our experience.

As a horse trainer, I am familiar with the power of the thoughts I think that influence the horse I am schooling. With time and practice, I have developed the capacity to consciously send through my front brain the exact picture of the movement I would like the horse to produce. When I see/feel clearly an impulsion-filled head to the wall leg yield, the pushing hind leg tracking well up underneath the belly, the horse's body supple and round, firm and forward in my hands, I experience just such a movement with the horse, moment by moment.

Concentration and focus broken, with the bark of a dog, the shout of a child, whatever, and it is back to mindfully, consciously, creating my front brain picture of desired outcome. Linguists tell us the power to transfer thoughts brings about subtle alternations in our neuro-muscular and skeletal structure. It is these infinitesimal somatic body shifts that trainers for eons have relied on to 'cue' their horses and teach new movements.

The Dalai Lama would have us believe there is more to this communication than words and somatic changes. His work suggests to me that horses possibly read our minds, a reality I am consciously choosing to live within these days, thus, it frequently forms my experience.   This principle always operates and is especially powerful when I fall out of mindfulness and revert to unconscious old programming. Let me explain with the help of one of my newer colleagues, Sea Sea Ryder:

> I first notice "CC" April, 1999, in Tucson Arizona, hanging out in a back paddock of Al-Marah Arabians' porta-stalls, as I moved back and forth readying my gear and my horses for the move to Prescott, Arizona. He nickered, and psychically called to me. I began pausing from my chores to engage him in conversation. Tammy, the breeding barn manager, told me the apprentices had started him, but his high energy, and short attention span proved too scary for the beginner trainees. So "CC" had been relegated to the back paddock until a decision was made about his future. She pointed out he was not likely to be sold, as he had a slight curve in one of his front legs. Such crookedness, while possibly never contributing to his taking a lame step, did not represent the best farm breeding.
>
> He captured my attention and focus; there was just something about his air and attitude that called to me.

I asked the farm manager for permission to explore his possibilities in the month I had remaining at the farm in Tucson. Given the okay, I commenced a basic regimen of grooming, groundwork, and longeing. A week later, I was in the saddle and thoroughly enjoying his huge stride. Yes, he did have a tremendous amount of energy and a short attention span. He reminded me of our adolescent attention deficit hyperactive disordered (ADHD) special needs students. True, he had been started.

He was at the 'turns like a rudderless ship' stage, with only stop and go full tilt.

The basic schooling figures of dressage in preparation for the pre-training and training level tests helped engage his mind. The goal of dressage is to bring to bloom and fruition the highest potential of the individual. Frequently switching school figures and lessons to channel his energy with new challenges, I was struck by his athletic brilliance.

Often, however, I found myself thinking of him as being "slow" in the mind department. I liked him. I liked the feel of him while riding. He just spoke to me. So even as he developed a huge abscess in a molar that required all sorts of high maintenance drugs and nursing, I accepted the opportunity to take him along to Prescott as part of the AIA herd.

In Prescott, we settled into our schooling routine, preparing for the busy camp months ahead. I continued to think of "CC" as mentally "slow". One particular day, when all 6 horses were under saddle by schooling staff, on a walk to the ball field and up the hill for conditioning, we passed a horde of **children**, third graders, tossing balls on the playing court. Steady crone alpha mare Rama was in the lead and found nothing alarming about the wave of **children** screaming "horses, horses" rolling towards her. Accepting Rama's read on the situation, the next horse in line, Vargas, continued sedately behind her. Next, came me and "CC" who alarmingly began to canter backwards, scattering these horses: Voo Doo, Missy, and Friar Tuck.

I had only read of a horse's ability to canter backwards. Apparently, this movement was included in the early

European high school tests. I was now experiencing first hand the extraordinary effect and feel of a horse quite intently going backwards at the canter. Sadly, "CC's" mind had departed elsewhere. He was oblivious of his path over Voo Doo, Missy, and Friar. The others kept their presence of mind and remained calm. Rama continued her cruising walk, followed by a surprisingly compliant Vargas. Eventually influenced by the calming energies of the group, we re-organized to continue.

In my mind, I was busy ruminating on the stupidity of this horse. "He isn't slow; he's outright dumb!" I thought. Failing to read the herd's calm, continuing-on-their-way attitude, fright sent him backwards at the canter. In our processing circle after putting the horses away, as we commented on our experiences and created schooling plans for next time, I expressed wretched judgment over my perception of "CC's" mental deficits. With gentle compassion, the staff suggested I practice what I teach. Petra, a staff member, wanted me to affirm "CC's" positive qualities. I was unable to comply. Give me some time with this, I requested, and we wound up for the day.

As part of my go to sleep ritual, I asked Holy Spirit for some help in perceiving "CC" differently. I was aware of missing the real horse, **lost in the pain of my judgment.** The next morning in our circle, as we made our verbal safety agreements and discussed what that meant for us, I said, "I'm Barbara and I agree to be responsible for myself today, and thus, contribute to the safety of the group. What that means for me today is to ask for support in consciousness from all of you that I remain mindful of my thoughts, especially those about "CC". To help me out, I awoke with a barn name ringing in my ears, **PROMISING.** From now on, I am affirming his promising qualities, his work in progress nature, and his extraordinary high energy and enthusiasm. "PROMISING!"

Months later, with mindful practice, frequently, very frequently, my experience of precious, precocious Promising is quite naturally, PROMISING!

5.   **Schwung:**   the power generated through the horse's hindquarters that travels through the back of both horse and rider, to deliver the desired movement.

This same connected power is accessed on the ground through **conscious awareness** of feelings flowing through mind/body/spirit during the heart scanning exercise, initial greeting, haltering, grooming, lead line work and the tacking process. Focused attention is essential. Mindful awareness focused through the lens of the human heart generates the connection—access to the TAO.

I would like to illustrate this particular principle with a true story occurring at Chapel Rock Retreat Center in Prescott, Arizona. (This Center, owned and operated by the Episcopal Diocese of Arizona, is open to guests of all faiths. The American Hippotherapy Association Board of Directors has met there for several years, as has NARHA's Health Education Committee.):

> At an **AIA** session with a group of 60's campers, my colleague Jack shared a very powerful insight. Our stated purpose was to practice elementary inter-species communication by filtering our thoughts through the lens of our hearts. We were consciously and mindfully slowing all our movements around the horses to half speed, while reverently listening with the feelings in our bodies. We were opening access to our intuitive channel for knowing; a sensorial capacity humans have allowed to lay dormant.
>
> After watching the herd of eight horses romp and play in the back paddock, several voiced fear. Many in the group were afraid to work around such large and powerful animals, especially because they felt they could no longer move about with the athletic verve of their youth.
>
> At that time, Jack admitted to not being a horse person. He had not been educated in the world of horses. He is a teacher of energy work at the collegiate level, and a master educator on how to follow and read energy. This consciousness on his part made him very safe around the horses. In fact, over the years of our working together co-facilitating **AIA** workshops and classes, he has become a competent rider. He never went through the 'passenger' phase of learning to ride.

Rather, from the very beginning he co-participated mindfully with his heart in speaking the "language of horse" – Equus.

This Equus energy language involves spending time reverently grooming and bonding with the horse. Consciously and mindfully, Jack readies himself and the horse for mounted work. The repetitive strokes of the grooming process, rhythmical massage, and Tteam work allows the principle of entrainment to produce a non-ordinary state of consciousness. Jack's biorhythms move synchronistically to match those of the horses.

Jack says to the horse, "You know more than I about this piece of work, so I'm going to sit here and concentrate on the pictures I'm creating in my front brain. I am willing to feel my feelings here and now. I know you read my mind, my spirit, my inner self. I'd like to have a safe, fun trail ride. Thank you."

Jack rides and works with horses mindfully, fueled with heart energy. He also interacts with people, while centered in his heart, mindful of the pictures he creates in his front brain.

Two women, both named Marilyn, had worked in the round pen with Ripple, the young half-Arabian pinto mare from Oregon. These ladies had spent time engaged in the bonding, grooming, and breathe-with process. The observing group grew excited, as they realized how easily they could read both the mare's and the ladies' commitment to sending clear pictures.

If the Marilyns were confused about what they wanted to see happen, then the mare's behavior was confused. Moments of focused clarity were helped by the observing group's support in consciousness. Both of the ladies, in their early 80's, experienced thrilling moments of connection.

The congruency of their expressed desire to have Ripple walk, matching their felt intention and focused picture produced Ripple walking. This was no easy feat for such a high-energy, kick-out-at-the-world mare.

In our insight-sharing circle at the end of our **AIA** session, Jack, in commenting on the bravery of both Marilyns and their work in the round pen, said he had been reminded of his recent visit home. Just a few weeks prior he had traveled to Washington to visit his Mom, who, at that time, was into full-blown dementia. His Dad was fighting the situation and was seemingly unable to accept what is.

Jack helped his partner Beth, and his brother, Bob through their initial interactions with their altered and confused Mom by teaching them the energy lessons of round pen reasoning learned during **AIA** sessions; allow time for the grooming and bonding process; send clear pictures in your mind; filter everything through the lens of your heart; listen with your feelings in your body. Intuition is a two-way channel. It is not affected by dementia. Jack 'round penned' his Mom. They had some fun with the alpha mare dance.

"What about your Dad?" the group questioned.

"He's not there yet!" responded Jack.

6. **Collection:** refers to the state of being "on the aids" in balance, harmony, grace, and oneness with the rider's preferences. Ease and flow dance movement lightness.

"Ease is the path of alignment."

Integral to the **AIA** process is the 100% full participation of all resent. Individuals may be participating in either observation/ perception mode or active/engagement mode.

Awareness consciously and mindfully noticed (without judgment) of feelings flowing through each individual consciousness present is the essence of this process.

A word about **processing:** This practice of sharing with others personal insights developed through experiences of similar activities or situations is viewed as an experiential learning tool. Its purpose is to anchor more firmly self-knowledge building metaphoric bridges for everyday life skills. For those listening to another's developing insight(s) while consciously aware of internal feelings in one's own body, opportunities to identify similar processes in one's own life with an alternative perspective (seeing in a different way) emerge. At the conclusion of each **AIA** session gathering, in the processing circle where the work originally begins, all in the circle, participants and staff make a statement of what it is they feel they learned. They are encouraged to discover how this teaching might generalize to their life at home, with family and friends, in school and/or at work.

The **AIA** Mirror Principle is my personal conceptualization of to practice these principles in all our affairs," as I studied a challenging passage in the Big Book of Alcoholic Anonymous. It occurs early in the text, "each and every time I have a problem with a person, place, or thing, the source of that problem lies within." Happily, today, what was once rough going is now a treasured truth: *"If I see it in you, it is also in me."*

When working with a new idea, thought, or concept, I have found it very helpful to practice an attitudinal shift. I pretend for 10 minutes that such a new concept, insight, or thought might be true. How does it improve, enhance or add to the quality of my life? This personal test for truth may prove helpful, as you explore the following ideas of **ADVENTURES IN AWARENESS.**

We work more with this principle in the section on the round pen reasoning, congruent message sending, freedom circle dancing and interactive equine facilitated psychodrama exercises. We will move through this handbook, much like we move through an actual **ADVENTURES IN AWARENESS** session. First, a few more theories for our conceptual framework.

TRUST THE PROCESS

The **AIA** model promotes the notion that the participant in sessions brings unique gifts of experience, talent and skills, while presenting some interesting challenges.

These challenges are best perceived as opportunities to engage the participant in interactive exercises with the horse for the purpose of gaining personal insight into their individual schematic of reality. While you may feel you have a fairly accurate "take" on any given situation with a participant, please remember to step back, ask the horse, and allow the process to unfold. **"TRUST THE PROCESS"**; the horse will clearly give you *and them* an accurate picture.

The story of Dundee illustrates the active initiative and co-facilitation demonstrated repeatedly by the sensitive empathic horses during **AIA** sessions. I believe these occurrences are particularly evoked *when looking through the AIA lens.* **AIA** emphasizes the horse or pony as an integral member of the co-facilitation team. "When in doubt, ask the horse."

During the summer of 1996, while facilitating a pilot project incorporating the **AIA** process into an Arizona Church camp curriculum, I had the opportunity to work with two remarkable Arabian horses, and two charismatic ponies, a POA (Pony of America) and a mixed Shetland/Welsh. The campers this particular week were older adolescents about to enter their senior high school year, or had already graduated from high school and were about to embark on full-time work, or were going to be freshmen at college.

The group of 18 young people this particular morning appeared frozen in their "hip, slick and cool" postures. They did not seem willing to fully participate. Yet, they were listening. Involved in their individual worlds, they had not yet connected to each other or joined in a group, as they groomed the four animals tied in a circle to a huge oak tree.

We moved to the round pen and the congruent message sending exercise. I demonstrated the significance of a focused mind, sending clear thought-forms fueled with conscious heart-energy.

Dundee, a young, attractive, 6-year old bay Arabian gelding pranced and danced around the pen; he appeared to delight in being admired for being his magnificent self.

Matching my deeply felt appreciation for a creature able to so easily display such joy and enthusiasm for being his best real self with my expressed message was easy. I discovered magical feelings demonstrating our connection.

We began to "join-up" and play with each other a short game of "cut the cow" (freedom circle dancing).

The group began to come alive, as the notion of frolicking with a large animal such as the horse took shape in their consciousness. When I requested one of them to join me, nobody wanted to be the first volunteer.

As the silence lengthened, Jason spoke up. "Is this something I can try?"

He created a positive surprise. Jason, blind since birth, was 17 years old. He went everywhere with his cane, and in new situations, a volunteer on his arm assisted him with the sighted-guide technique.

"Of course," I responded.

A staff person assisted Jason into the arena and acted as his sighted-guide, helping him move through the exercise. His enormous willingness to participate fully in the experience of interacting with Dundee, regardless of how foolish he might have appeared in his awkward efforts at a new activity (never mind, the young man being blind), and his bravery for trying began to excite his observing peers.

The group grew quiet and attentive as Jason demonstrated moving Dundee out to the rail at a walk, a trot and a reverse. Then Jason paused and disengaged himself from his sighted-guide assistant.

"This is pretty flat even ground, isn't it?" he inquired.

"Yes. We've put the pen on a sandy ball field." I replied.

"Well, can I try it alone? Just walking around by myself?" he asked.

"Okay," I answered.

We stepped to the center and allowed Jason freedom to move around the pen. He dropped his cane intending to move around freely, on his own. Now, the group became very still. Dundee, at a halt on the rail, eyed him curiously.

Jason was stumbling. He was not practiced at moving freely about on strange ground alone. Dundee moved in next to him and placed his withers in the same position on Jason that a sighted-guide assistant would take. Each time Jason stumbled, the horse moving next to him, provided his body as balance.

"Look," called out one of the boys. "That horse is acting as Jason's sighted guide."

And, indeed, Dundee stayed at Jason's elbow with his withers exactly placed so Jason could balance himself and not fall. Together they walked, they jogged, and they ran. They did circles and figure eights together. Many of us were crying.

There were clamors of, "Jason teach me how to do it," and "I want to try."

Jason became the peer coach for the others, as they took turns in the round pen with not only Dundee, but with Voo Doo Dream, Tops, and Alf as well.

At the end of our session, 18 individuals had come together and formed a group, coaching each other in feeling okay about the awkwardness, as they helped one another learn a new and challenging FUN activity.

BELIEFS AND THE INTERNAL PROCESS

Most people are unaware of what it is they believe. Our beliefs significantly influence the development of our interpersonal relationships, especially with self and God.

Discovering self and our relationship to a power greater than ourselves (represented metaphorically by the horse), contributes to the quality of relationships we form with others in our lives.

Oftentimes, people are not familiar with internal processes and the mechanisms by which "unconscious beliefs" contribute to their personal experience of daily life. Recognition of preferred communication or information processing style(s) can be a first step toward internalized awareness - knowledge promotes empowerment. Working with a large animal such as the horse, *archetype* for power develops awareness of personal power. Learning to work effectively and safely with unpredictable power (the horse) allows an individual to internalize this skill and become comfortable with - power; authentic empowerment contributes to healthy behavior choices, thus contributing to reduced societal violence.

Being responsible for self, mentally, physically, emotionally, and spiritually, while working with the horse and its instinctual nature as prey species, contributes to enhanced personal comfort with one's own instinctual nature, especially the prey (victim) side. The prevalence of domesticated dogs and cats may indicate a higher degree of comfort within out culture for the predator (perpetrator) side of our instinctual nature as humans. Indeed, look at our fascination and support of body contact sports, scary movies and violence-fraught media.

Befriending a large prey species such as the horse, learning to work easily and comfortably around and with it as archetype for power promotes the development of personal power. Authentically empowered people find it easy to live in balance, harmony and peace with themselves, the environment and others.

Often our personal communication is colored by acculturated distortions (the polite lie) that inhibit our expressed truth. The horse is quick to reflect discomfort when there is lack of congruency. Horse trainers know that a horse grows resistive and agitated when it 'reads' the individual as unaware of what they are truly feeling inside, or thinking, unconsciously. The horse makes no judgments about these thoughts or feelings. It wants the comfort of authenticity, an energetic matching on all levels - mind, body, and spirit. The horse reflects like a mirror an individual's thoughts or feelings with its behavior. As a prey species, the horse wants to experience, with the human handler, a matching of energy, both expressed and felt. The horse is **always reading** us our spirit, our energy, our inner self. Yes, the horse is a mind reader.

Many of us are unaware of what we are thinking. Most humans do not consciously recognize when they are operating from a **prey** (victim) orientation or **predator** (perpetrator) orientation. Humans are unique in our capacity to be both prey and predator. With practice, consciously, mindfully, we are afforded the opportunity to experience integrated brain function. We can develop our consciousness and achieve balance—neither prey nor predator—balanced peace.

I believe such consciousness in today's world takes skillful practice and an intense intentionality of focus. The horse gifts us with a remarkably clear picture of how we are doing with our efforts to achieve congruency, which is the first step toward inner peace. The horse reflects back to us its 'reading' of our inner messages. Too often, the civilized adult is unconscious of their internal landscape. Unaware of their inner conversations, they are sometimes dismayed with the horse's behavior and refusal to cooperate.

People come to **AIA** sessions to learn interpersonal relationship and communication skills, while developing expanded awareness and insight into their personal process - experience of life. The language of Equus provides metaphor and symbol, much like dream work. An individual's capacity for intimacy may be reflected in the mirror of horse's behavior in the congruent message sending exercise.

My empathetic 'emphatic' colleague in equine facilitated experiential learning process work is Voo Doo Dream, a 1987 Arabian gelding, bred by Al-Marah Arabians in Tucson, Arizona and owned by Roxanne Green. Voo Doo has worked as an equine experiential educator in **AIA** for about seven years. He is practiced in the art of mirroring to humans aspects of their interior—psyche's many facets. He embodies the qualities of 'trickster—clown' and is often mistaken for a mare with his lovely face and lithe body.

One day seated outside the round pen at Al-Marah, I watched the congruent message sending exercise, as Marcie worked with Voo Doo Dream. She struggled to release her horse trainer personae and follow the dictates of her heart. Marcie's challenge was to filter her thoughts, feelings, emotions, assessments, and evaluations, through the lens of her heart. She was tasked with letting go of her mental template of round pen training. Once firmly anchored in her heart space, she was empowered to choose consciously her action.

In the shade of the mesquite tree, outside the **AIA** round pen, I found myself on the edge of my chair. I was watching, through the filter of my own 'stuff' – myself. The picture unfolding before me represented me, my raw edgy feelings. Before me played out my ineffectual attempts to break out of an ancient mold, an unconscious picture of how I thought 'it' (deep intimacy with a beloved) had to or ought to look.

Voo Doo sought connection with Marcie. He actively engaged her at every turn of his head towards her, ears attentive, eyes alert, and nostrils quivering, flared in question. Marcie was in her trainer mode. Keeping up a continual patter on his movement quality and his equine psychology, she was oblivious to his emotional feedback. She was missing his attempts to engage her on a more intimate subtle energetic level.

After well over a decade of equine facilitated experiential process work, I KNOW that horses have volunteered to co-create with us the next evolution of interconnected inter-species life on Earth. Healthy interdependence is our current lesson.

My heart turned over and my body-mind poured out heated energy in the form of deep muscle - bone pain. Fiber tingled. There was me. How much I missed, as I was thinking I was so attuned. Yes, thinking. Mind involved, but not connected, not at home in my heart-body, willing to feel my feelings.

"Time out," I said.

Marcie stopped, came to the rail and dropped her longe wand, as she rested her arms on the rail. "I can't seem to get him to turn into me," she said.

Our colleague, Clyde, volunteered that he was still observing Marcie in her training role. He did not see her working out of her heart.

Marcie paused, and expelled a frustrated breath. She spoke of her efforts to discover her new role in life. What was she to do, now that her son is grown and leaving home? She was feeling without purpose. Finally, with tears openly flowing, "I don't know how it looks or feels—living or acting from my heart."

Did I mention Marcie is a brilliant medical scientist with many beneficial discoveries to her credit? Life lived anywhere but her mind is virgin territory.

"Breathe and connect your mind-heart-body," I said. "Really notice Voo Doo with your heart-body."

The gray gelding had picked up the longe whip and was gently tapping Marcie's shoulder with it. "Let's try this again, he's saying," I hinted.

Marcie laughed, "Okay." She returned to the center of the freedom circle, closed her eyes, breathed deeply, grounded and centered herself. When her eyes opened, Voo Doo had placed himself in front of her. Slowly he moved into her, chest against chest, his head resting on her shoulder. Spontaneously her arms surrounded his neck and they embraced in a heart hug.

My own heart was singing. Perhaps intimacy doesn't look like any picture. Maybe it's allowing oneself to slip into the flow of life energy, surrendering to what is, in an attitude of reverence and magic— celebrating MYSTERY. Thank You Voo Doo Dream.

BEGINNING A SESSION

How is it that the **AIA** model contributes to expanding awareness and developing consciousness, and how might this prove problematic with participants? Let's begin with the initial introductory curriculum.

Prior to actually engaging in an **AIA** session, participants are asked to fill out some paperwork. This **application requests** permission to treat in the event of an injury, information on medications, and any current life changes: i.e. job changes (new boss, new co-workers), recent moves, relationship stresses and/or breakups, health challenges or concerns, loss of a loved one, etc. Rarely do people remark on the changes occurring in their present life or comment on their unconsciously "asleep at the wheel" cycle of living. This question on the application appears to be viewed negatively. Change is perceived as difficult, fraught with challenges and issues.

AIA staff members fill out this application at the start of the session along with the participants. The co-facilitators discuss the current changes in their own lives. All of life is change. Opportunities to learn, to grow, to accept, to re-perceive, to let go, to grieve, to create, to implement, to dream, to vision, to imagine are the heart of life's cycle. At any given moment, we all have significant changes going on in our lives. This question is meant to pique thinking and feeling, to establish an inner dialogue before gathering in a circle to commence the process. Only later do people remark that, in retrospect, there are several significant changes occurring in their lives at the present.

Likewise, people rarely answer the question about medications, with any conscious accuracy. Vitamins, supplements? Caffeine intake, diet sodas, smoking. What about compulsive TV watching? Radio? Is there an inability to be alone with oneself in a quiet house, or alone with oneself in nature, quiet, still? Is there excessive activity, over booked social calendar, constant phone use, shopping, eating, gambling, sex? The point is to look with care at the ways we avoid feeling our feelings.

Every **AIA** session begins with gathering in a circle. It is our routine for grounding and focusing, centering our energies as we move to work with the horses. For some, this may feel threatening. Levels of discomfort may range from having had a bad experience in group therapy to not having sat in a circle since Kindergarten. Some individuals are uncomfortable with the circle being closed or with the circle being left open to the east to encourage enlightenment. With no barrier such as a table, notebook or pen, the touchy-feely closeness of human bodies may be overwhelming.

Highly empathic individuals, those who feel the feelings of the whole group and struggle to sort out what is truly their personal authentic feeling, do require extra support in consciousness. The safety agreement is permission for them to turn inward and notice for self their personal boundaries. Truly sensitive to the energies of the entire group, the empathic individual may be encouraged to observe the herd, locate the horse who might represent them today, at this moment in time, and study with care the horse's behavior in keeping itself safe.

SAFETY AGREEMENT & CENTERING EXERCISES

I can hear the comments now on the breath-centering exercise for ADHD (Attention Deficit Hyperactive Disorder) clients, behavioral acting-out adolescents, or even oppositional/defiant adults. Quiet sitting in a circle not possible? You may be surprised.

For high-energy days, be creative. We have circle-danced in parking lots (Flagstaff Riding Club), as children trooped off a bus chanting our verbal safety agreement in unison, picked up on rhythmic clapping, finger snapping of a nervous adolescent acting out, and unified the group with invitations for them to teach us a centering exercise. We have learned chants, rap dances, rhythmic movements of the martial arts. Youth are enormously creative when given permission to express what is *real*. **An AIA principle is celebrating our differences, accepting what is, and allowing the process of group interaction to unfold.**

In the circle, verbal safety agreements are made and participants are invited to share how they feel at that moment by naming an animal they resemble. It is important for each participant to express what this safety agreement means to him/her so that the group is clear as to why they are saying it. The safety agreement is **"My name is _____ and I agree to be responsible for myself today, and thus contribute to the safety of the group."**

While most youth and adolescents have no trouble with the notion of centering and breathing exercises (there are those who giggle, and that is okay), the adult participant may be stretching emotionally to even close their eyes. When the facilitator talks about "attuning to feelings freely and fully felt in their uniquely designed, preciously perfect bodies... bright beautiful mind in service to their wide open, compassionate heart... feeling connection to center within self...," these may be alien concepts to the adult participant.

At the completion of the centering activity, many people report significant emotions rising to the surface. The circle may be experienced as a forum for being heard, giving voice to emotions, thoughts attached to feelings. The feeling of no judgment and no need to fix allows for release, an opportunity to let go. Acceptance of what is becomes a healing experience.

Crying in public is generally not easy for adults; crying at all may be impossible. As much as the facilitator may create safety emotionally for the experience of crying, it is often not okay with the adult participant. Native American healers teach that human tears are essential. The negatively charged, electromagnetic energies of tears help to cleanse our environment. With tears there is a general systems cleanse physiologically removing toxic wastes emotionally, physically, mentally and spiritually. Tears caught in the back of the throat may be extremely uncomfortable.

Permission to fully feel and to express feelings is the heart of the AIA process. It is primary to the safety of all working around and with the horse. One of my journal stories is an excellent illustration of this issue of adults and crying in public. One of the individuals in this story is the Dean of Agriculture at a large southern state university. It is early summer, 1994, and a colleague invites me to assist with teaching the **AIA** equine facilitated experiential learning process work to her class of student psychiatric nurses.

> The Agriculture College gave us permission to work with their 80 resident horses. I spent the morning before the day of training with the barn manager. My purpose was to recruit equine volunteers to participate in the training. Each of us equipped ourselves with a halter and lead line. We toured the pastures, engaging the residents in conversation.
>
> Seven horses followed us back to the barn led by Jake. Easily 30-plus years, Jake was a mere shadow of his magnificent Thoroughbred heritage, yet, he carried himself with regal poise. Our halters were still slung over our shoulders. They had not been necessary.

The barn manager, in reporting to the Dean on the process of horse selection, was heard to remark: "We walked out into the fields and she asked for volunteers. Seven followed us back to the barn, led by Jake. We didn't even use the halters!"

The Dean told her he would attend the initial opening of group the next day. He had to meet this 'female horse whisperer'.

During the opening group circle, the Dean made it clear that in his world horses are a commodity. They are money on the hoof, work and market animals. No higher consciousness of the lower animals, according to his scientific world-view. He did listen to the stories and reflections, expectations and feelings of the student nurses, the volunteer safety support staff of pony club members and their teachers, and me, the **AIA** facilitator. He decided to stick around for the bonding portion... and then the grooming... and then... the opening round pen segment.

Jake had indicated to me that he was to work first. Yet, when loose in the deep sand of the training round pen, he rolled, and then strolled over to hang his head over the rail, not near the group who had groomed him. No, Jake's focus was on Susan and her mother, Molly, the local pony club coach. Susan, a high-level dressage rider for the region's Young Rider Team, was scheduled to compete in Chicago that August.

"Just great!" I'm thinking. "The one time it won't work is in front of academic disbelief."

Jake is not to be budged from his position attempting to nuzzle Susan through the bars of the round pen. Occasionally he would bump Molly, but his attention remained focused on Susan. Puzzled, I suggested that Jake wanted Susan and her mother in the round pen. So in they came, equally baffled. Jake immediately put his nose on Susan's chest and anchored himself, so Molly did the horsewoman thing, and began inspecting him closely.

Now, Jake's body had seen better days. The barn manager mentioned he was a 'gift'. He did have a lip tattoo, faint and hard to make out. He was suspected of being well over 33 years. Molly was busy going over each leg.   Jake kept his nose on Susan's chest.   She began stroking him, remarking on how faintly similar his ancient face was to a horse she had once known.

Suddenly Molly, who had reached the off hind leg, began exclaiming, "Susan, Susan, this isn't Jake.   This is 'Tripper'; Trip the Wire!"

"What is going on?" I'm asking myself.

Molly set the off hind leg down gently, and returned to face Susan and Jake.   She was openly crying.   "Susan, this is your first horse.   TRIPPER.   It's him.   I'd know that scarred pastern anywhere.   That starting gate accident is the reason we were able to acquire him.   He taught you to ride!"

"You were four years old when we got him.   And seven years old when I leased him to the neighbors to teach their little girl.   When we moved, I lost track of him," Molly continued.

Now Susan was crying, I'm crying and, as I looked over at the spectators; they too are crying.   Even the Dean.   He stayed to close our AIA circle.   He was suffused with emotion and unashamedly tearful, as he expressed the opening of awareness he had experienced this day.   He admitted to not feeling clear about the scheme of things, yet profoundly newly aware that horses have consciousness.   They are not money on the hoof; they are sentient beings, with heart, spirit, feeling, and memory."

Postscript: this same large agricultural school is now home to a therapeutic riding program.

Safety Agreement Centering Circle at TROT in Tucson, AZ

Some of the AIA herd at Aim High Equestrienne Center in Tucson, AZ.

Bonding during Hat Ranch Adventure workshop in Williams, AZ

More bonding at Hat Ranch Adventure

Mutual choosing at Aim High in Tucson, AZ

A Further mutual choosing at Chapel Rock Retreat Center in Prescott, AZ

Centering with practice feeling bioenergetic field.

Con Su Permiso - notice presence of red shaped Heart upper
portion of photo....days after Vargas transitioned to other side.

Heart Hug with "Maple", AM Village Maypol

Con Su Permiso and feeling the field with "Rama", Ramblin-Kay-Bar

More Con Su Permiso with Rama

Grooming VooDoo Dream at Al-Marah Arabians in Tucson, AZ

Group grooming with Serra June at Chapel Rock in Prescott, AZ

Crackers and participant in round ring - tending gestalt at Hat Ranch

Imaginary Lead Line at Horse Power in Temple, NH

Dick and Mingus in Eugene, OR – game of hide and seek

AIA developmental feelings process with Serra June at Hat Ranch

Developmental feelings process with VooDoo at Chapel Rock in Prescott

Trust Walk in Sonoita, AZ - Silent Integration

AIA Schooling rider at EquuSatori Center, Sebastopol, CA working Johan

Shasta at Sierra Tucson Hospital in Catalina, AZ
chatting with Vargas and Mr. Fabulous.

MOVING OUT OF THE COMFORT ZONE

In the opening circle, "time out" calls are explained. If, at any time, an individual is feeling uncomfortable, mentally, emotionally, physically, spiritually, they agree to call a "time out". When hearing the words "time out", everyone agrees to pause, take a deep breath and notice fully where he or she is in relation to the horses and to each other.

It is at this point that many adults require a reminder that it is not possible to be wrong. There is no way to make a mistake during an **AIA** session. Facilitators and safety support people only intervene to redirect activity and/or horses' energy for the sake of safety. When the statement: "You cannot do anything wrong in **AIA**" is made, sometimes participants are confused as to what this means. The intention is to assure participants that unless it is a safety issue, anything you do is okay. This is a very difficult concept for most people to grasp.

Many adults have become so ingrained in their thinking that someone else or something else is the cause of their discomfort (victim orientation) that it takes conscious practice to be responsible for the content of our thoughts about someone, or something. Our thoughts color emotion and contribute to our experience of reality. Considerable concentration and internal willingness is required to shift one's perception into recognizing that choice for how we think and what we think is possible. Equine facilitated experiential learning is an opportunity to practice this challenge by choice.

"Challenge by choice" is a phrase designed to remind the participant that an awareness of personal choices available empowers an individual, as well as group process. **AIA** sessions encourage conscious stretching of internal boundaries either through informed decision-making to move out of one's comfort zone and fully participate as an "active observer", ready to give feedback about personal perceptions, or through active moment-by-moment engagement.

What do I mean by the phrases: conscious of internal beliefs? Stretching internal boundaries? Expanding a personal comfort zone? Allow this 'Story of Ollie and Become Tree' to illustrate.

> At this particular **AIA** session, we were investigating the influence of our thoughts on surrounding energy. We tested our capacity to influence the strength of another human being. First we encouraged scattered, even negative thoughts as a volunteer, Betsy, stood in our circle with upraised arms. Todd pushed down with some energy to eventually cause the lowering of her arms.
>
> Then, we consciously sent positive energy through our heart, just as we do when we initially scan the horses in the paddock to discover which horse is to be our teacher—our bonding partner. Betsy experienced a feeling of increased strength and stamina in her ability to keep her arms upraised as Todd again pushed down. Todd reported a higher degree of difficulty in causing her upraised arms to lower (muscle testing).
>
> So what of Ollie and Become Tree? Some years ago during an Intermountain Center session at Therapeutic Riding of Tucson (TROT), in Tucson, Arizona, we were engaged in a game of fox and hounds. Three Native American youth, high school aged (SED - Severely Emotionally Disturbed) and I deliberately 'ran away' down the Tanque Verde River wash-a broad open expanse of dry riverbed, surrounded on both sides by a Mesquite Bosque.
>
> We were still in the open plain when the group chasing us started down the bank in our direction. The TROT horses, well practiced in this favorite game, tracked our progress with their extraordinary senses. Their ears had a direct fix on our location. Ten minutes head start and the 'hounds' could barely fail to see us.

We were on open plain, a fair distance away, exposed with the lack of vegetation. There were only two small mesquite trees a short distance away.

Ollie suggested we move over to one of the skimpy trees, hunker down, and be still. Ollie was quite persuasive and we followed his coaching. Now we were in plain sight of the approaching eight horses, their mounted riders, my assistant credentialed instructor, and safety support volunteers. Ollie continued to coach us.

"Become the tree, breathe and become the tree." Ollie's voice was rhythmic and hypnotic. He was chanting melodically, "Become the tree; breathe and become the tree."

Amazingly, the entire group passed by. They were quite a distance beyond us when Ollie broke the spell by beginning to whoop and holler.

Years later, this memory is poignantly fresh. I feel, at a visceral level, the ease and lightness with which the four of us cloaked ourselves in the garb of one skimpy mesquite tree. We became tree. I learned a very powerful reality-altering lesson from a tremendously interesting young man. I am glad I trusted my instincts and surrendered to his teaching.

Work with horses provides a clear precise mirror of our inner thoughts, feelings, attitudes and beliefs (our internal landscape). The horse is not concerned with judging the content of our thoughts, feelings or attitudes. The horse simply wants us to be aware of what it is we are thinking and feeling.

Adults who have never probed the area of the mind where thoughts are read by the animals are truly uncomfortable with the notion of "no privacy". Giving permission to play with the idea of this truth (as if on a Star Trek episode) for the duration of the session is often effective. Most youth and adolescents, especially those in treatment or active in the detox process, are quick to point out this is not imaginary.

THEY KNOW WHO IS COMING

Anchored in my personal belief system is the idea that the horses engaged in this work of equine facilitated experiential learning (EFEL) and equine facilitated psychotherapy (EFP) know and expect the individuals who appear for a session. They have agreed to share a particular gift of awareness, trigger a personal insight and/or evoke a deeply buried feeling. **I believe that this mutual work of interaction, mindfully fueled with heart energy (compassion), is bringing both horse and human to another evolutionary level of consciousness.**

This belief is reinforced each time a group moves from the circle to the mutual choosing exercise and heart scanning. While still in the centering circle, participants are coached to become aware of their breath, to straighten their spines, to plant feet firmly on the ground, and to move from focused vision to "soft eyes" (seeing out the edges of your eyes-peripheral vision). Any thoughts are moved to the heart with the mind's eye where they are filtered through the lens of the heart in a search light arch of energy extended outward toward the horses. It is often helpful to suggest the image of a rainbow bridge of heart energy arching out from one's chest like a beam of light.

Participants proceed to the fence, accompanied with the suggestion to carefully approach each horse (usually remaining on the outside of the fence), and heart scan — mutual choosing exercise.

Instructed to notice the feelings flowing through their bodies as they engage each horse in this fashion, participants are likely to feel an internal 'Aha' when connected in this way to the horse also choosing them. We each have unique and different ways of recognizing our internal 'gut' response to truth. AIA sessions are an opportunity to practice continuous mindful noticing of this personalized internal truth mechanism. Learning to listen, honor, and accept the wisdom of our body's messages affirms our mind/body/spirit nature. This is the essence of equine facilitated experiential learning process work.

People are curious as to what it might look like when a horse chooses them. How does this process work? The following story demonstrates this perfectly.

> In July 2000, a group of Spirit Horse participants at the Horses of Hope facility in Baxter Springs, Kansas, (Horses of Hope staff, volunteers, Crawford County Mental Health Services staff, and students) circled up in the afternoon for a second session make-up group. Valerie, head instructor for Horses of Hope, explained that the horses the group usually worked with had all worked a full morning giving mounted lessons and they were on a well-deserved break, turned out on the 20-acre pasture north of the barn.
>
> "Big Red and Doll are ready to teach developmental vaulting this afternoon," Valerie continued.
>
> I caught Valerie's eye and mentioned the possibility of Friar, Voo Doo, and Rama, three of my AIA horses, being available for developmental vaulting.
>
> "And some of Barbara's **ADVENTURES IN AWARENESS** herd may choose to work as well," Valerie said brightly.
>
> The young group of intense students, mostly boys, ages eight, nine, and ten, with various severely emotionally disturbed diagnoses, talked about recent activities in their lives to bring the new volunteers and the visiting Colorado student intern up to speed. Each carefully made their safety agreement, while reading the group designed rules. "I agree to be responsible for myself today and thus, contribute to group safety". The rules: KEEP IT SAFE, HAVE FUN, COMMUNICATE, TAKE TIME OUT, AND BREATHE.

Valerie reviewed how the process of developmental vaulting and practice on the barrel would proceed once the horses had been chosen, groomed, and tacked with pads and surcingles. She explained the significance of group support and observing quietly, while awaiting each person's turn, and the role of the safety side walkers who were selected based on trust.

The group trooped out to the back fence line where there was not a horse to be seen. There were 20 acres of grass pasture, a flowing creek, and a lovely pond shaded with huge oaks, maples, and pines. Jimmy suggested we listen carefully. "Da Dump, Da Dump, Da Dump, Da Dump."

As we heard their hooves pounding the dirt bank, still obscured by huge trees, I caught a glimpse of Vargas, his liver chestnut body bleached out by intensity of Kansas summer sun.

Vargas was leading the **AIA** herd at a strong gallop followed closely by Rama, Friar, and Maple. I was just wondering about the rest when Voo Doo and Sea Sea Ryder crested the hill to slide down the bank and negotiate the creek.

"Oh my," I said to Shelly, director of Horses of Hope. "I forgot the 'Big V'!! His favorite people are active boys in this age range!" "Oh buddy, how could I?" I exclaimed, as he cruised his 17.2 hand body by me, snorting, to plant his huge Roman nose on the chest of a young man leaning across the wire to stroke his liver chestnut coat.

Valerie was laughing. "Well, I guess your herd wants to work with this group!"

And in the magical way of this work, the boys chose Rama, Friar, and Voo Doo as well. The four horses fit and schooled for developmental vaulting with young **children** showed up out of a 20-acre pasture on a hot summer afternoon to do what they do best - demonstrate and give unconditional love and acceptance.

"How did these horses know we wanted to work with them?" asked one of the younger girls.

"How did they?" echoed Crawford County Mental Health staffer, Kelly, who with her blond luxuriant hair both resembled and had the same name as Kelly, owner and bonded partner of Vargas. She was busy rubbing the ears of the Big V.

"What made them come?" she asked with wonder.

Inside I was feeling warmth flood my heart. I was imagining the late night phone call to daughter Kelly, telling her that once again her partner played his role in the AIA process. I gazed into the fathomless depths of Vargas' large, brown eye. Great Mystery looks back. I know. HE/SHE LOVES.

MUTUAL CHOOSING

Many people are convinced that they are not going to be chosen. They are sure that they are the exception to the rule. Or, they are unable to get past their personal belief system (their individual template of reality) to briefly experience this other dimension. All of us have a special sensory, advisory feeling referred to as intuition. Intuition alerts us to danger. It struggles to reach our consciousness prior to an 'accident'. Some people voice-feel intuition in their heads. Some feel a tingling sensation up and down their spine. Some have the hair on their neck and arms rise. Some break out in goose bumps, even on a hot day. **Our bodies do not lie to us.** Many of us have varieties of all of the above and experience varying intensities according to the level of the message's urgency or significance. The more we become practiced in honoring our sense of **intuition,** the clearer the message(s).

I have witnessed horses move toward a participant, extending their heads to nuzzle and touch, seeming to wrap them into a body hug, as when a mare brings her foal in close to protect, and pushing other horses or people out of the way. I have watched horses follow an individual down the fence line to meet them at the gate. I have observed horses bump people from behind in an effort to elicit attention. It is surprising how many adults are unaware of being chosen. They are either not tuned in to their own attraction or not familiar with that mutual 'Velcro' lock-on feeling.

Professional instructors often question the AIA practice of allowing participants to "mutually choose" their own horse for the initial student/teacher portion of the session. Traditional wisdom dictates the correct and educated pairing of individual horse to rider as crucial to successful and safe experience learning to work with and ride horses. We will discuss more about this process when we review the teacher's text accompanying the five-day AIA curriculum. For now, know that I am not suggesting instructors throw away their professional training and safety practices. Rather, I want to suggest another perspective that allows for the 'feedback' and 'input' of our colleague the horse. I believe that DIVINE WISDOM flows through the horse's interactions with humans and that our task is to open ourselves to the lessons of these gifts.

After more than a decade allowing the horses to choose their participant teams, I have come to recognize DIVINE INSPIRATION at work in these pairings. The personal insights developed because of these, often unlikely, partnerships continue to delight and amaze me. Frequently information surfaces that releases long held energetic blocks to open awareness and feelings of joy. From the summer of 1998 comes the following story, which demonstrates, clearly, inter-species communication. People are curious as to what it might look like when a horse communicates with them. How does this process work? The story of 'Vargas Speaking English' illustrates a possible version of the student-teacher inter-species communication process:

> Wednesday morning's group of middle school campers at Chapel Rock were seated around the rail during an AIA session. Three of the boys had mentioned fear was an issue. One had fallen off a horse on a trail ride and broken his arm. Another had been run over by a bolting horse. Yet, another said his best friend had been really hurt by a horse, so he was afraid to get too close, much less ride.
>
> Several of the girls, more interested in the up-coming dance that evening, were hanging in the background, talking about possible choices of clothing for the evening. These girls kept saying that horses didn't like them. I found myself looking for a kind way to say, "And how much of the horses' not liking you is really you not liking the horses?"
>
> Searching for some breathing space and not wanting to voice my thoughts, I walked out into the paddock where Voo Doo was busy eating a tree.

"Don't do that little buddy," I said quite loudly for the benefit of the observing students. "We've an agreement that you won't kill off these lovely shade trees". I found his 'soft' spot and began to knead it with my fingers. He stretched with appreciation and fell into his camel neck, quivering lip pose.

The herd (all eight) clustered around listening to me chat with Voo Doo and his girl friend, Lizzie. At that time, five of the AIA horses were purebred Arabians, both geldings and mares. Two of the others, a paint mare (five years old) was 7/8 Arabian, as was Crackers (18 year old gelding) whose other eighth is Welsh pony.

"Ok you all, lots of fear as well as dis-interest in this group. I know you're sensing their hesitancy, but I need for you all to stroll over to the fence and engage," I said with a final pat to Voo Doo's neck.

Shortly, I was followed by all eight horses; Vargas in the lead, cruised up and down the fence; he appeared to be a horse with a mission. Leif, our assistant instructor, said, "Look, 'Vargie' is choosing his team".

Vargas placed his huge head in the lap of Zachary, the boy who had been stepped on and had expressed the most fear. Vargas just stood there.

"Do you feel like you've been singled out?" I asked.

"Well, I guess so. This is hard to ignore," Zachary said. He was busy scrunching back in his chair away from the huge face against his chest.

"Well, rather than backing up and trying to move your lap, consider asking him to move his face," I suggested.

"Horses don't speak English," the group responded almost in unison.

"Or do they?"

Vargas pulled his head back through the rail and went to the boy with the fear of breaking a bone. Again, he pushed his head through the rail and into John's lap.

"Am I being picked too?" questioned John.

"What do you think?" I asked. John's face was alight with a shy smile of delight.

Once his selection was acknowledged, Vargas again removed his face and went to the third boy who had expressed fear and dislike of horses. "Yes, you too." he appeared to be saying, as he stuck his head into the seated boy's lap.

"Well then, that's the Vargas group," I said to the gathering youth.

I turned to address my talented colleague.

"And who do you want as a safety support staff person?" I inquired of this wisdom-filled sentient being.

Without hesitation, Vargas moved back down the rail, pushing Ripple and Lizzie out of the way, to clearly indicate he was also choosing Kristin. Kristin's face illuminated with recognition; that feeling of connection - mutual choosing.

"Hey," said one of the now quite interested girls, "that horse speaks English."

Later during the closing circle, the boys were asked what gift Vargas gave to them. "If he (Vargas) really does speak English," I inquired, "What would he be saying to you?"

"We're the coolest dudes!" responded John and Lenny.

"It's okay to say you're afraid. In fact, it helps to talk about being afraid. The power goes out of the fright," said Zachary.

As the boys left for lunch, Vargas positioned himself at the gate and nickered. Each boy patted his huge Roman nose goodbye. "Thank you Big Guy - You're the Coolest Dude!"

SAFETY DEMONSTRATION AND BONDING EXERCISE

Once student/teacher agreements are made and the group, as a whole, is clear on which horses have been chosen and which horse each participant is bonded to, and who is the safety support person for their chosen horse, the riding instructor (horse expert) gives a brief demonstration on how to safely approach a horse and how to work around the horse in a group. Elementary equine psychology and physiology principles are covered. The equine range of vision, other senses, nature of their non-integrated brains are reviewed (instinctual response system of flight/fight, freeze, faint). The basic theory, "a horse is a horse first", the flight and fight response is discussed as possible metaphor for human fear reactions.

Procedures to keep everyone safe are explained, such as not walking in front of a tied up horse; walking safely behind, either by giving the hindquarters a wide berth to avoid the kick zone, or by walking close to the haunches, touching the horse on the rump; and everyone staying on the same side of the horse. The proper approach to a horse is demonstrated by moving on a diagonal toward the horse's withers, while being alert to their attention and focus on you and your movements, as you move into their energy field.

Participants are taught to observe the horse's ears, their facial expressions, the licking and chewing signals, pooping and gas passing responses. The practices of asking permission to approach, con su permiso, using your voice to introduce yourself as you ask permission to stroke their neck, withers, and perhaps chest is also part of the safety lecture and demonstration.

These safety demonstrations and grooming lectures are a good opportunity for your program student interns to work practicing their teaching skills. It is very important for all staff and volunteers to "model" focused attention on this activity. Do not allow this safety procedure to deteriorate to the level of the flight attendant's request to check out the safety card in the seat back pocket of an airplane.

The activity of grooming and how the implements are used is reviewed, affirming that the goal is to utilize the activity of grooming to engage in developing relationship. The horse getting clean is a by-product. The rhythmic, patterned movements, working in the horse's etheric energy field, produce resonance to the horse's biorhythms. Stream of consciousness processing emerges out of this repetitive, mindful activity. It is this entrainment of the human's biochemistry to that of the horse, that I am currently investigating. This "era three", Dossy, MD 2000, shared mind invokes access to sensory perceptions not ordinarily available during daily activities.

Groups develop confidence and trust, as they assist each other in interpreting the horse's body language. The designated safety support person for an individual horse reminds participants to phrase their suggestions in "I" format. "When I see. . . , I feel. . . , or I think. . . , or I sense . . .". As the work progresses and the groups come together in their grooming and bonding process, the co-facilitators move from cluster to cluster observing, alert to each horse's response and communication. Questions such as "What drew you to this horse?" "Are you aware of others in your life that might be like this horse?" "If this horse spoke English, what message might he/she be giving you?" help to stimulate the participant's thought processes.

Adults are often self-conscious about speaking aloud to an animal in the company of others, especially if they are around people they do not know, and thus, do not trust. The facilitator may coach the safety support person to allow each individual sharing a particular horse to have individual one-on-one time, stroking and grooming, mindfully aware of the thoughts and feelings flowing through their body. Expressing aloud such thoughts and feelings assists with bringing to full consciousness material that may be new to awareness or altogether unfamiliar. At this time, awaiting team members practice their observation skills, reflecting on horse's body signals and checking out their perceptions with the horse's safety support person.

For the facilitator, close observation of this initial *gestalt*, interaction of horse and participant, presents a valuable picture of an individual's preferred processing and communication style; the way an individual takes information from their environment and runs it through their body/mind processing contributes to their reality base. An important point to remember with anyone, but particularly with adults, is to 'meet them' where they are; access their belief system and initiate a dialogue within its parameters. AIA does not seek to change a person's beliefs. The **AIA** process **does** focus on bringing to conscious awareness those beliefs currently in place.

There is clinical evidence to suggest that regular, repetitive, patterned stroking on the horse's nervous system (grooming, Tteam, massage) produces non-ordinary states of consciousness in both horse and human. Focused-awareness and mindful-acknowledgement of messages expressed through feelings in the body, while conscious of the horse's body language may produce access to material not usually available in ordinary consciousness. At the physical level, such neural plasticity is known to influence brain regeneration. Human biochemistry is altered. Homeostasis prevails.

The principle of entrainment operates as the biorhythms of human and horse move into synchronization. In this light alpha brain state, material from the unconscious emerges and is expressed both in a verbal stream of consciousness, and in the somatic movements of the participant's body.

The stream of consciousness process is illustrated in the story about Adieu that occurred at Sierra Tucson Hospital in Tucson, Arizona, in early 1992:

> While I'm not happy to report about this 'dumb' thing, I did, out of the resulting events a major breakthrough happened for a young girl, 14 years, an elective mute, and a suspected victim of major abuse. The very next day she was scheduled for transfer to a higher acuity level facility and was only in the barn to 'hang-out' with her psyche-tech aid. One of the regular adolescent boy's group was in session with a visiting psychiatrist from Mexico City as a guest participant.
>
> With such a large group, we had divided interest levels, and the instructor was working with a mounted

skills class in the arena, the barn manager had a small group for round pen work, and I was working with several boys and the psychiatrist on ground driving Adieu.

Things were going well with this lovely seven-year-old bay Arab gelding. Everyone, including the psychiatrist, had practiced long reining at walk, halt, and for some a trot about the gravel stable yard. We decided to hitch Adieu to the jogging cart.

In an effort to make the harness fit, I tied knots in the tugs to shorten them. All was well, as we circled the stable yard at a walk, but when moved into a jog - ah well, you get the picture. Ugly! The rim of the jogging cart bumped Adieu's hocks with each stride. Now, most horses would have hit the road for the next county. Not this sensible, alert therapy horse. **I felt like he could see my thoughts through the reins.**

Adieu picked up speed in an effort to escape the pain of the bumping jog cart. I struggled to quell my growing sense of panic, as I searched for a plan. Stopping him with a whoa was out of the question. He truly bordered on frantic flight into another dimension and could not hear the aid to stop. We were now circling the stable yard at a tremendous clip. Tip over? Or . . .

I glanced up and saw the fire hydrant near the activity center building. "Hit the fire hydrant with a wheel and break the harness free," I thought. However, I did not want to be in the cart now headed at a canter-into-gallop pace for this exact hydrant. Again, I felt Adieu read my thoughts. I leaped from the cart ten seconds before its right wheel impacted the hydrant.

I was sliding on my belly over gravel, head up (I did have a hard hat on), to see the harness break and Adieu gallop free. Trailing traces, his speed slowed, as he circled the barn. He did not head down the open road; instead, he circled the barn and, slowing further, trotted into his stall.

The psychiatrist ran up to me crying that this is why he went into psychiatry. He faints at the sight of blood. The boys gathered round, picked me up and helped me get into the barn and the wash rack. My clothes were in shreds, and the blood from the gravel scrapes was flowing. The barn manager brought Adieu to one side of the two-stall wash rack; and I was in the other.

The boys and psychiatrist were hosing me down while Adieu was being rinsed off after his shredded harness was peeled away by the barn manager and the 14-year old girl who had moved in to assist with the horse. She began to stroke and calm him.

The barn manager showed her some elementary Tteam strokes for calming and gentling. As this young girl worked on the horse, she began to speak. The psychiatrist moved in closer and heard her say, "He's not in his body. He's done just what I do when my dad comes into my bedroom at night. He's away - out somewhere else." She continued to work on the lathered bay horse. The psychiatrist continued to hose me down, as well as listen to the young girl pour out her heart. Unselfconsciously, she told her story to Adieu.

After a time, the horse shuddered. "Look. He's back!" she said.

Accompanied by the psychiatrist and the young girl, I walked to the nurses' station for my own first aid. And yes, a follow up meeting with my supervisor. Not pretty.

Postscript: This young girl was not transferred. She remained in treatment and designed her ITP (individual treatment plan) to include working with Adieu.

BREATHE-WITH EXERCISE

During the grooming and bonding period of an **AIA** session, further, intimate connection is possible when the participant mindfully attunes their breathing to that of the horse. Beginning with a hand on the horse's withers and one on the horse's chest, the participant gently rests their ear next to the horse's skin. Sometimes this step is preceded by a mutual breathing into each other's nostrils (horse and human). Careful observation of the horse's flank reveals the inhalations. The participant begins to breathe with the horse's breath.

For me, when I do this exercise, I feel like a melting into or fusion occurs with the horse and me. Boundaries of body disappear and I know oneness. Students have told me that when they observe me demonstrating this exercise, the stillness of both the horse and me is awe-inspiring. Upon completion, I feel refreshed, filled with energy and aliveness. The horse and I appear to dance and sparkle with radiance.

I believe there is a significance in the choice (often unconsciously) of horse with which to demonstrate an exercise. I am not yet able to prove my theory that we attune to the horse's energetic pattern; much like a Stradivarius violin masterfully played in purity will set to vibrating a similarly tuned violin located in another portion of an acoustically superior room. In the past decade teaching, facilitating, and participating in **AIA** sessions throughout this country and in Europe, I have both observed and experienced this attunement. I concur with Dr. Andrew Weil's message that expanded consciousness and increased awareness contributes homoeostatic balance within our mind/body/spirit.

DRAWING THE ENERGY EXERCISE - IMAGINARY LEAD LINE

When teams have become comfortable with the grooming activity and have been given the opportunity to breathe with, one-on-one, the safety support person instructs each individual on proper leading of the horse. The most stressed rule is not to allow the lead line to become wrapped around the handler's hand or any other portion of the body. The participant holds the lead at about 8 – 12 inches from the halter snap with the right hand and holds the rest of the lead in the left hand.

Participants practice leading the horse, walking and stopping, circling both directions, up and down the fence line, remaining aware of the other arena traffic. The individual participant practices with the horse, while supported in focus and attention by other team members.

As facilitator, I know when a group is ready for the next step in this exercise by watching the teams. The energy of the group's interaction demonstrates the strength of their bonding. An invisible network of connection is illuminated. Are they focused on each other? Are coaching, help and support readily supplied? Has an individual's success with the activity become a group effort?

Once the group demonstrates bonding with the horse and the horse demonstrates acceptance of this human herd, the notion of the invisible lead line while doing this same activity is introduced and practiced. With several such groups working at once in a generous sized arena or paddock, it is advisable to keep halter and attached lead line on the horse. Loop the lead line up around the horse's neck and secure with a half hitch safety knot under the neck (easily pulled loose).

This portion of the interactive exercises introduces actual practice with support in consciousness, power of intention, and clarity of unified purpose. It is important for each group member to have an identified, agreed upon role. One person on the right, one on the left, or maybe two on each side, depending on group numbers. One person is designated to 'draw' the horse/energy, positioned slightly in front, maybe two to three people in this tip of the triangle position, this 'lead' sets the pace for purposeful movement.

A goal is discussed and set before beginning; perhaps it is simply to walk as a group (horse included) toward the fence, or corner, or tree, or middle, or whatever. Once the groups become practiced in trusting that the horse is part of their group, or they, as herd, are able to move about with a conscious group will, the fun begins and laughter rings out. If a group is having trouble, suggestions by the safety support person such as, "don't look back; look to where you want to go and **trust** the horse will follow." Emphasis on trust is important since oftentimes this element is lacking in a person's life. As they become more trusting of the process, they will become more trusting in their personal lives.

Horse people will recognize the psychic stretch involved for the horse. A horse is inexorably drawn to be part of a group of horses. It prefers horses, its own kind, to people. Yet, regardless of a breed, (okay-Arabians excel at this exercise); the horse will disregard its instinctual attraction to the other horses and surrender to the bonded groups' collective and purposeful plan.

Again, participants are reminded that nothing they do in **AIA** can be wrong. A story from my Sierra Tucson Hospital medical staff training in late 1991 illustrates "just is".

> The head nurse of the DAE (diagnostic, assessment, evaluation) unit was working in the round pen with Deva, a young, four-year old, chestnut, vibrant, flirtacous mare. Chris, a big man – 6 feet 2 inches and 225 pounds, was frustrated in his attempts to send the energetic half Morgan, half-Arabian out to the rail. He was tapping quite vigorously on her hocks with the longe wand, his voice authoritatively signaling her to "trot".

Deva was planted, immobile, not moving. She eyed him. Minutes before she had, in demonstrating with me the basic body language concepts of free longe work, displayed the fire and energy inherent in her nature. Quick and responsive, we had played a short game of cut the cow.

Our barn manager's husband, a long time horseman and cattle rancher, was filming this medical staff training. Standing on a hill filming the events, the tape's audio was rendered unplayable because he was repeating into the microphone, "I f...ing don't believe it. I f...ing don't believe it. Horses don't f...ing behave like this!"

He was dismayed at the incongruity of a horse not moving away from stimuli and very vigorous stimuli at that. And Chris, in the round pen, was brought to tears when I inquired, "What in you really doesn't want to send this mare away?"

"She's just like every other woman in my life. Lovely, pretty and won't listen to a thing I say!" Chris had dropped the longe wand and was searching through his pockets for a nonexistent tissue. Deva turned and stepped toward him. She actually curled him into her, as a mare would hug her foal. Tears fell freely; this large man admitted he truly just wanted her to go with him.

"What would that look like? I asked.

"Well, I'd just go and she would come with me," he responded.

"Okay. Just start walking," I suggested.

Chris gave Deva a long slow, lingering stroke on her shoulder and proceeded to walk. Deva moved right out with him. They walked about freely, together, for some time.

ROUND PEN REASONING – CONGRUENT MESSAGE SENDING

During an equine experiential learning session, I seek to avoid mentioning that in the hospital and clinic setting, this interactive exercise is known as equine facilitated psychodrama. Before getting underway, it is important for all participants to agree to keep their focus on the individuals in the round pen. No side conversations. Stay alert to the feelings flowing through your body, and consciously move to your heart filter any thoughts you may be having about the *gestalt* unfolding before your eyes. Focused attention on the activity in the round pen, while simultaneously remaining aware of the feelings flowing through the body, allows the active observer/ participant to consciously access personal internal material.

The active mode or the observers' mode Participant/Observer Principle) becomes conscious choice. The essential nature of both elements for collective (shared) reality to exist is experienced. Quantum physics theory suggests that in the act of observing, that which is observed is 'colored' by the observer's lens (filter of material that makes up an individual's current consciousness). The intention of the observer to see a particle of light rather than a beam of light allows the observer to see the particle. A shift in intention to seeing a beam results in seeing a beam.

Further, quantum physics postulates that in order to perceive, that which is perceived must first be named. Adults in the audience of an equine facilitated psychodrama are inexorably engaged in their own feelings process, as they watch gestalts in the round pen.

Asked for feedback, adults begin to practice owning the source of their observations, their internal landscape of feelings, thoughts, beliefs and attitudes.

Feedback is phrased very carefully to reinforce self-responsibility in "owning" one's perceptions. This practice contributes to acknowledging that the ultimate source of what we perceive in the world beyond our eyes originates first in the world behind our eyes.

Phrases such as, "When I see _____, I feel or think __ _____. Is this true for you?" - serve to help the participant become conscious of self, the inner observer, as powerful originator of perception. The result is authentic empowerment.

Opportunities to express these personal insights occur during the formal "time outs". The person in the round pen working with the horse may become stuck, request help on what is being seen by the audience, ask for suggestions and ideas, or just want support in consciousness. The story of Mingus and Dick illustrates this process:

> During the summer of 1995, in Eugene, Oregon, 3-day rider and trainer Ted Reed hosted the **ADVENTURES IN AWARENESS** workshops at his lovely Belle Tour Farm. Ted's mother, Carrie, offered her retired field hunter, Mingus, as one of the **AIA** horses. The group members, this particular day, were from Healing Bridges, the recovery outreach and advocacy program, directed by Meira Yaer, RN, MA, for adults with brain injury.
>
> We created a round pen in a squared off section of Ted's indoor ménage. The barrier across one end of the arena was constructed out of various jump standards, poles, and barrels. The audience, in folding chairs, was seated on the perimeter of this equine facilitated psychodrama theater. During the Student/Teacher - Mutual Choosing portion of the **AIA** process work, Dick had chosen to engage with Mingus. They had formed quite a palpable bond.

A word about folks with brain injury: frequently extraordinary sense and perceptual skills, abilities we all innately possess, manifest and magnify because of the rehabilitation experience. Some group members reported 'seeing' the energy between Dick and Mingus.

Questioned about what game he wished to play with Mingus, Dick responded immediately with "Hide and Seek".

"Oh, okay, that's a new one to me," I said. Privately, I'm thinking, "and a new one to the horse as well."

"What do you mean, hide and seek?" I questioned.

"I mean I count to ten and go hide in that back corner. All hunkered down. And Mingus comes and finds me," Dick replied.

In my head, I'm thinking, "Yeah, right, sure."

"Okay, let's work with that," I said.

Now, Mingus is a cribber. He is powerless to resist the inviting temptation of the wood poles and standards. Mingus is not focused on Dick. He is busy feeding his addiction – his need to suck air by biting on wood.

Two separate times Dick stepped to Mingus' head, requested verbally that he play with him the game of hide and seek. Dick voiced his expectations. He would go hide in the corner where he wanted Mingus to come over to him, as he waited, hunkered down.

For those of us watching, it truly seemed as if Mingus received and even agreed to the picture of Dick's request. But addiction is a cunning, powerful, and baffling situation. With the second attempt, it appeared momentarily that Mingus would indeed turn away from the attraction of the poles and go find Dick.

No, sadly, cribbing prevailed.

"Time out," I called. I asked the group how many had played this game. As children with playmates - All. Could we bring into our conscious awareness, present time the feeling quality of playing hide and seek? Could each individual member of the group agree to hold in their current conscious awareness (their front brains) the imaginary picture of Mingus turning away from the poles to go find Dick? Each individual verbally agreed to participate, actively picturing Mingus going to find Dick.

So, again, for the third time, Dick went to Mingus' head and verbalized his request. He would go hide in the corner. He would be counting aloud to ten, as he moved to the corner to 'hide'. He wanted Mingus to come 'find' him, to come over to him in the corner.

I felt like collectively we held our breath, as Dick went through the ritual for a third time. Dick never paused after making his request. Counting aloud he headed for the corner and hunkered down.

Mingus tracked his movements with his eyes, yet swung his head back to the poles. He opened his mouth to bite the wood and. amazingly, he stopped - mid-bite. Mingus turned and looked again at Dick. Then, he looked again at the tantalizing pole.

Huge sigh. Mingus snorted.

The group let out its breath in a whoosh.

Mingus turned and **trotted** briskly over to the dark corner to "find" and nuzzle the waiting Dick.

This story not only illustrates the power of support in consciousness; it also illuminates the dynamic of our continual interactive process with each other. Our thoughts our feelings, our attitudes, our beliefs contribute to our personal construction of the reality we experience daily. It is my belief that becoming conscious of this process in ourselves develops self-empowerment. Authentically empowered individuals live in peace and support of one another and the planet.

DEVELOPMENTAL FEELINGS PROCESS

The **AIA** developmental feelings process utilizes the activity of the different developmental positions, as in classical Hippotherapy, on the back of the moving or stationary horse, to provide the participant with a non-ordinary state of consciousness. The resulting stream of pre-conscious awareness artfully mirrored by the horse's movement and body language contributes to self-developed insights. Frequently cathartic release of emotional blocks occurs.

Mindful rhythmic supported steps in the bonding and grooming activities together with intentional breath, and attentive focus of facilitator and team (side walkers & horse handler) serve to influence biochemical brain wave activity of all participants on the team. Most particularly, the mounted individual moving through the positions assisted by the horse, horse handler, side walkers and facilitator discovers access to Psyche's interior.

AIA's developmental feelings process is a culmination of the inner-active and interactive exercises previously discussed. **AIA's** grounding inneractives of centering, heart scanning, mutual choosing, con su permiso, imaginary lead line, grooming, round ring gestalts and congruent message sending are the foundation for the capstone workshop – **AIA JOURNEY RIDE**. This subject is explored in depth in book number two: **AIA JOURNEY RIDE**.

During the **AIA** workshops, the **AIA** facilitator(s) initiate, within the boundaries of the round pen's deep sand, the conscious choice by the participant, of their developmental feelings team; two side-walkers, horse handler, and horse. This team creates a safe mounted work ambience making a conscious agreement to remain fully present in their bodies – "holding the kite string" (Grof/ HOLOTROPIC Breath Work) for the mounted participant. The others present serve in the active/observer witness role. The circle of the round-pen or arena space provides a container (Jung); a cauldron for alchemical change.

The horses who volunteer to participate in the intensity of this work mirror the deep inner psychic processes of the participant. Sometimes this immense energy is frightening to those not familiar with unconscious emotions cathartically expressed. At this level of consciousness, certain exceptional horses have agreed to co-participate in this process work, consciously bringing into awareness from deep well of Psyche material long hidden and now ready to be resolved and integrated.

"Trust in the process" is the facilitator's function. Focused attention is the role of the horse handler. The horse transmutes, with its enormous presence, the participant's emerging feelings fully felt. Having journeyed this path through direct experience of his/ her own developmental feelings process, the **AIA** facilitator remains fully present to the participant's needs. Concurrently, the horse handler, equally familiar with this developmental feelings process through their own practiced experience, remains fully present to the horse's needs. The story of Voo Doo Dream and Ellen illustrates this process:

> Ellen was seated astride Voo Doo Dream, who was, at the time, a 10-year-old vibrant gray Arabian gelding, with several years experience working in both EEFL and EFP sessions. Ellen had chosen her side walkers from amongst her fellow participants during an **AIA/EFEL** residential training workshop. A professional instructor and advanced dressage rider, she was enjoying the elementary vaulting positions.
>
> Ellen had chosen her horse handler, also a fellow student, as an intentional exercise in consciously expanding her trust level. She was seeking to enlarge her circle of peer associates with whom she might share openly what was true for her. Ellen was not a native of the US and often experienced difficulty in feeling fully understood.
>
> Sharon, the horse handler for Voo Doo Dream, an experienced professional horsewoman who directs her own riding program in the Midwest, had spent some

time walking Voo Doo in the elementary lead line and bonding exercises to affirm their connection and communication.

Now Ellen was expressing delight with the current activity and feeling trust with the side walkers who first provided hip lock security (similar to full treatment team Hippotherapy model) and then stepped away when she was comfortable without them. The group was making large figures in the round pen at the walk when the facilitator asked a probing question: "What about the way you are feeling now? Can you carry this feeling with you as you return to your work environment?"

Ellen responded almost immediately, effusively rattling on about her feelings, plans, thoughts, and hopes. Voo Doo stopped. Sharon urged him forward. No, he was planted. He refused to budge. Briefly, Ellen's dressage instincts kicked in. She firmly nudged Voo Doo's sides. He remained immobile.

The facilitator stepped in. "Are the words you are saying the ones you think you ought to say, feel, and do rather than feeling what really is true for you?" inquired the AIA facilitator.

Ellen burst into tears. Nothing she was saying was true for her. It is what she thought she ought to feel and believe. When Ellen gave expression to her deepest wants, feelings, fears, and desires, Voo Doo moved off in a smooth air-glide stride. Unasked, he simply moved into a flowing walk, as Ellen spoke her truth.

Each time Ellen did not express her truth he stopped. Planted, he refused to budge, as she searched deep within herself. Gradually, as she became practiced at asking herself what the truth for her was, Voo Doo glided forward.

At the end of an intense session, Ellen slid down to heart hug Voo Doo and her teammates. Clarity through expressing her truth suffused her face in radiance. Ellen expressed gratitude for feeling so validated in her "realness".

The group expressed its appreciation for the experience of her willingness to share with them her real self. Laughingly she said, "I had to be true to me, or Voo Doo wasn't moving."

"And can you take this feeling of being true to yourself with you?" The **AIA** facilitator queried.

"You bet. To move forward, I tell my truth. First, and always to myself.   And I choose with care the people I trust to hear me."

The theory basis for both the **AIA** developmental feelings process and **AIA** JOURNEY RIDE can be found in the writing of Stan Grof, MD.   His cartography of the mind's non-ordinary states of consciousness and the gifts inherent in developing and expanding personal awareness contributes to an understanding of the inherent concepts.   An individual's ability to trust in feeling their feelings fully, while   experiencing a non-ordinary state of consciousness in which material from deep within their psyche is given voice, picture, sound, and action, promotes healing integration.

Both the **AIA** development feelings process and **AIA**'s Journey Ride incorporate a wellness perspective, mindful meditation, sensory integration, and equine movement patterns to produce different states of consciousness.   Andrew Weil, MD, speaks of the documented link between spontaneous healing occurrences and non-ordinary, or shifted states of consciousness.

The purpose of the **Adventures In Awareness** Internship Program's (**AIA** IP) core curriculum of 14 days of training in professional facilitation skills (aka HAT RANCH ADVENTURE), TASTE of **AIA**, Relationship Energetic, Equine Perspective and the optional capstone - **AIA**'s JOURNEY RIDE is to prepare the clinician, educator and horse professional to offer this equine facilitated experiential learning process work merged with their particular gifts, talents, passions and strengths.

The **AIA** IP curriculum is designed to be taken along with the Enrichment Menu choices over the course of 18 months to three or five years.   Core faculty members in these initiating years are myself, Ann Alden, MA, long time co-facilitator of **Adventures In Awareness** workshops www.llazyeranch.com) and Lisa Walters, Director of EquuSatori Center in Sebastopol, CA.   www.equusatori. com

AIA Workshops focus on relational horse skills enabling the participant to acquire a thinking practice for assessing safety issues;   to develop assessment, evaluation and processing skills; to internalize being responsible for self; and to discover and practice communication (including inter-species communication) techniques.

These workshops are open to the individual interested in personal growth and development. One need not be enrolled or even interested in becoming an **AIA** IP certificate holder. For **AIA** -IP students interested in obtaining graduate or undergraduate credit through the University of Arizona's Educational Psychology Dept. payment at the instate tuition rate is available.

Returning to our **AIA** developmental feelings process discussion, I have discovered, on a personal level, that when an individual is ready, the experience appears. No one is exposed to material that they are not ready to process. Some Higher Order of Wisdom is at work in the round pen during an **AIA** developmental feelings process session. It is the task of all present to respect and hold in reverence these energies. No judgment. What is, is. NAMASTE (The Light of Spirit in me greets the Light of Spirit in you).

Nothing comes to the surface of awareness and consciousness without this mutual readiness factor. Allow the story of Crackers, Clickers and Morphic Resonance to explain the notion of "when the student is ready, the teacher appears."

Crackers, a 17-yar old gelding, was again assisting me with the Chapel Rock Retreat Center's summer program in equine experiential learning featuring the (**AIA**) model. It was mid-July 1998, and one of our guests was Terri Arnold, nationally renowned professional dog trainer from Freetown, Maine. Her mission was to investigate the **AIA** process for possible use in her dog training camps.

During the previous afternoon's session, when a summer cloud burst necessitated 'alternate plan B', Terri succeeded in prying open my unexpectedly closed mind on the subject of behavior modification techniques. Like my quick take on synthetic saddles – and even more quickly revised, I was forced to expand my thinking, as I observed the effectiveness of Terri's work. Her clicker training of Vargas to hold his head down and steady to accept the application of eye ointment in something less than four minutes was amazing!

This training technique that is fun, non-invasive, and simple to master easily captured my attention and respect. So, the next morning I sought her help with Eagle. A registered Arabian gelding, AM Bachelor

Button, Top 10 at Second and Third Level Dressage at Arabian Nationals, at 21 years is an experienced EFEL/EFP colleague.   Together with Crackers, Eagle was on loan from The Riding and Rehabilitation Center. Located in Tucson, Arizona, it is directed by Ann Alden who mid-wived Crackers into the world.   Eagle was present at Cracker's birth and they are very, very best friends.

We were working with the clicker to teach Eagle to hold his head down and steady so that someone   from a wheelchair might easily bridle him. We were   in the round pen with about 500 feet between Crackers and us who was stabled in the back paddock, behind the house, out of view of the round ring.

In the beginning of our training session with Eagle, Crackers was still in the paddock behind the house. At about the point where Eagle had connected the pushing of Terri's fist with healthy pressure to obtaining a plain hay pellet from her other hand extended outward away from the clicker, I suggested to the other participants and Terri that morphic resonance is not just a theory; it is a fact.

Emphatically, I told the group that Crackers, behind the house, in the back paddock, now knew this trick. The theory developed by British scientist, Rupert Sheldrake, promotes the notion that sentient beings with attuned consciousness are capable of remote viewing – sharing learning and knowledge.

To prove my point, I suggested we might test for truth through Crackers. I requested my assistant bring him from behind the house.   Mary went to retrieve Crackers, and Terri continued with the training of Eagle. She transferred the reinforcement of the clicker/ hay pellet to shaping the desired behavior, gradually extending the length of time Eagle kept his head down and lowered.

Mary returned with Crackers and tied him to a tree some distance from the pen, as we demonstrated the stage Eagle had reached.

"Bring in Crackers," I said. "I know he now knows this trick."

"Absolutely no way," said Terri. "It's not possible."

As Mary led Crackers through the round pen gate, he was not even halfway through and he was reaching for Terri's fist, pushing with firm pressure, and then swinging his head to her other out stretched hand for the pellet. Terri exclaimed, "This isn't possible!"

Three consecutive times Crackers pushed her fist to receive a pellet. Then, **he offered the desired behavior, a lowered and steady head.**

"No way. This can't be. But it is! I'm experiencing the impossible – as truth," exclaimed Terri.

"Welcome to **ADVENTURES IN AWARENESS**," was my comment, smiling.

AIA'S EQUINE EXPERIENTIAL LEARNING: 5-DAY SESSIONS

Procedure: A group (8 to 10 participants, plus 2 adult accompanying staff) comes to the barn prepared to interact actively with a variety of horses and ponies. The first session (minimum of 3 hours) is devoted to establishing this process and to introducing safety guidelines and practices. Basic equine psychology and physiology are reviewed. Participants wear sturdy, closed toe shoes (no sandals – tennis shoes are okay) and long pants. People attend **AIA** rain or shine.

Process: At the beginning of every session, participants are seated in a circle. Introductions, basic safety and housekeeping process are reviewed. A short centering exercise focuses the group's energy. At the completion of each session, time is allotted for the group to re-gather in the circle and explore insights while planning the next session's activity. Ordinarily the curriculum is the following basic outline; however, there is enough latitude within the structure of each session to accommodate equine and participant input and suggestions. Horses co-facilitate **AIA**'s equine experiential learning process. All in the group, this includes adult accompanying staff, **AIA** staff, student interns, and volunteers are perceived as both students and teachers.

Session #1 -- Participants should not expect to ride the first session. Seldom is mounted work part of the initial gathering. There are a tremendous amount of safety practices and equine psychology principles to cover, as well as the mutual choosing, Con

Su Permiso, grooming, lead the energy, and bonding work with the horses during the first session.

Session #2 -- begins and ends as outlined above, as do all the sessions. Major work during this session is the Con Su Permisio, congruent message sending exercises and round pen reasoning process.

Session #3 -- is devoted to the triad teaching teams and includes mounted work in the form of introductory developmental vaulting. This is foundational work of the **AIA** developmental feelings process used with adult participants. Some in the group may choose to work further with freedom circle dancing (more on this later).

Session #4 -- resembles a traditional skills development lesson. May include trust walk – in silence with side walkers, horse handlers, and safety support spotters.

Session #5 -- is goal oriented towards "taste of the trail" and games. Ceremony of Completion. Spirit Horse Painting. Rain activities include game of stable PICTIONARY, Tteam work, and some of the John Lyons calming cues, long reining, training videos.

STEP-BY-STEP 5-DAY CURRICULUM

Step #1: Schedule one-half hour before and after each 3-hour teaching session so the staff can gather to share personal needs for support, concerns, ideas, and thoughts about the group.

Step #2: Prepare the teaching area and staff.

Discuss with staff and practice the verbal safety agreement: *"My name is _____and I agree to be responsible for myself today, thus, contributing to the safety of our group."* Talk about personal significance of this responsibility contract. What or how such consciousness applies currently to self?

Form a circle with the chairs, or have room on hay bales for everyone in the group to sit.

Each horse has its own grooming box equipped with hoof pick, soft brush, stiff brush, currycomb, and mane and tail brush.

Horses' halters are well fitted with lead lines capable of being tied up for the imaginary lead line exercise (safety tie around horse's neck).

Horses' headstalls are equipped with snaffle bits, and the reins are equipped with snaps for ease of transfer to the halter during the first several lessons in skills development – sometimes known as a side pull.

Cavesons are removed from the headstalls as the halter is worn under the bridle to serve as safe attachment for the lead line during first mounted work and thereafter as required.

All horses working in program have been schooled regularly by the staff at walk, trot, and canter. They are familiar with being ridden bareback and have been schooled to the warm up exercises of arm circles, and riders lying prone and supine on their backs.

Designate a safe tie area easily seen by safety support staff and instructors. There should be plenty of room for groups of people to work around the horses. Remind staff and yourself to leave the tied horse an "out". All participants work on the same side of the horse. No one goes under the tied rope. A horse may pick up its hoof to flick desert sand up under its belly (for fly control) and unintentionally knock a person silly.

Acquaint staff with location of first aid supplies, location of telephone for emergency call, directions to the facility, and keep on location the participants' applications and emergency releases in case treatment is needed.

Mandatory: Instructor and at least one other staff member hold current certification in CPR and First Aid.

Practice with staff the drill for when a rider falls off. Know who on staff is responsible for what. Be sure horse staff know and are familiar with all collaborating center/facility policies and procedures. Schedule time with Director for an orientation.

Determine which pads, surcingles and bareback pads fit best on which horses and fashion some sort of marking system for participants.

Specify an all herd turn out area for energizing and bonding exercise. Spend training week with horses turned out as a group doing the energizing and play together prior to staff schooling work.

Staff schooling and training 5 days of the week for 4 hours per session, the week before horse skills week begins.

For 12 participants (8 to 10 youth with accompanying adults) plan on working with six horses. The purpose is to learn communication and interpersonal relationship skills as *relational horse skills are* learned and practiced. Designate two or three additional horses as back up in the event of burnout, lameness, or general malaise.

The instructor should include these back up horses in the staff schooling and familiarization program, as well as herd turnouts. Plan frequent consultations with collaborating program's barn manager to determine horse's health (mental, emotional and physical), as well as suitability to work, as prior efforts in other sessions may be an issue.

DAY ONE: The first day is the basic format, using the circle for feelings check, safety agreements, housekeeping arrangements, and review of the day's curriculum. Each participant introduces himself or herself when saying the safety agreement and the instructor identifies staff and details their roles. Discuss the concept and purpose of "time out" and what to do when one is called. Stress the significance of an individual who feels uncomfortable, is not sure of the next step, is not feeling heard, etc. and honor the participant being responsible for self and calling a 'time out' when needed.

Acknowledge a "time out" may be called by staff to bring the group to attention around some safety concern, or more likely to alert participants for the move to the next exercise. Be prepared for someone in the group to test their ability to be heard through exercising a call of "time out". Take it seriously. You are modeling for the group your commitment to being present for the horses, for the staff, and for the participants.

Remember that the participants acutely observe all staff interactions. The subliminal learning quotient is enhanced as compassionate healthy communications are observed and recorded. You hold the key to learning to work comfortably with a large, powerful, unpredictable, and sometimes frightening animal. Younger folk accord you the reverence of a goddess – god. Anchor this trust and continue to earn it.

Do some sort of centering exercise focused on breath and its significance for grounding into body while riding and working with horses. Movement stretches with breath help prepare for the energizing and bonding portion. Do not be concerned if a participant chooses or is chosen by a horse that ultimately you sense may be inappropriate for them to ride (perhaps there are height and weight concerns or incompatible learning and skill levels). At this stage, the lesson is developing relationship, accessing communication patterns, and determining learning styles – auditory, visual, kinesthetic, and experiential.

After the centering and focusing exercise, have participants stand outside the arena fence while staff energizes the herd with longe wands to keep their bodies a safe distance from the horses. Encourage the participants to utilize their observation skills and notice the ways the horses respond to the gyrations of the staff, as well as engage with each other in relationship.   Coach the participants to notice where their attention is drawn. Which horse holds their focus?

Once horses have been selected and teams formed of horse, participant, and safety support person a short safety lecture is given, with a grooming demonstration. The instructor remains unassigned to float; this role ought to shift between staff members after the first 2 days, when instructor is alert to reading the energy of the horses interacting with their groups.

Participants are taught **Con Su Permiso**, the mindful approach to the horse, with reverence for a sentient being of consciousness offering teaching and learning gifts. Elementary principles of the energy bubble surrounding all sentient beings are discussed and practiced. Spend some time discovering your own energy and then that of another.

Work with simple practice of hands together as if in prayer knees bent, spine straight, long slow belly breaths, soft eyes with intentional noticing of feelings between one's palms. As sensations increase gently and slowly, pull your hands apart as if molding taffy or holding a balloon. Sensations of heat, cold, tingly are individual ways of feeling our surrounding subtle energy body. This layer of sentient being anatomy is information rich. Practice first on each other and then with the huge heart rich energy bubble of the horse's field.

Basic equine physiology and psychology are covered referenced to developing classical equitation skills, meaning the **balanced seat.**

Emphasize "challenge through choice". In the case of fear, participants are encouraged to go as far as they can, breathe, and stay in the moment with their feelings. If available, a safety support staff person goes one-on-one.

Allow plenty of time the first day for grooming, bonding, and general "hang-out" time with the horses. Have the groom boxes filled with some extra 'fou fou' items such as rubber bands for braids, ribbons, and hair gel for styling efforts.

Demonstrate and practice correct leading and safe handling techniques. Discuss the picture the front brain sends and how the horse accurately reads energy of intention, fueled with front brain picture of desired outcome.

It may be that participants have difficulty with the concept of the horse reading the picture their front brain sends. It may serve your purpose to illustrate with the circle to square game: Tie bailing twine (or a rope) together long enough for each participant to hold an area of the twine (or rope) without touching each other. Lay it on the ground in a circle. As they stand around the circle on the ground, have them contract to keep their eyes closed, or use blindfolds. They then reach down and pick up the circle of twine and move the twine into a square, while talking about how they are going to accomplish this task (all with their eyes closed). Talking is allowed. However, you may choose to silence individuals who are so loud that others have no opportunity to give voice.

Call out "Okay" to signal the successful move into a square. Spend some discussion time allowing participants to express how it felt to trust the process, to listen, to speak, to see inwardly the group forming a square. Mention that this process is similar to the imaginary lead line, and all work with horses and others in our lives.

Begin the grooming process, as outlined previously. After the grooming process, participants can practice leading the horses, and when they are confident with that exercise, move to the imaginary lead line exercise. Discuss traffic safety, awareness of their group and groups around them.

Give a ten minute warning prior to closing the sessions so participants can say goodbye, put grooming boxes away, help scoop poop, neaten the work area, and circle up for processing, insight developments, and thoughts about the next day. Generally allow 20 minutes to a half hour for insight development and processing for the purpose of firmly imprinting the life skills developed during the session. Stress the practical function of new skill or insight in daily life.

DAY TWO: Repeat of day #1, including review of basic safety while working around and with horses. Outline the plan for work in the round ring learning the freedom circle dance once the grooming is complete. Again, do not be concerned about the horse mutual choosing teams.

At the round ring, set the behavior rules of listening and looking and observing how the work is done, while noticing interior feelings. Discuss how feed back is given, "I see you... I feel... ". Ask what the horse might be saying, if in fact he/she spoke English.

Elaborate on the longe wand (whip), its use and purpose. Stress its role as both an energizer and a reminder to keep self a safe distance from the horse's body when the work is in progress. Steve White, professional horse trainer, tells me he teaches his students to work with the whip through the cardboard box exercise. A box is placed on the ground and the student is directed to move it about, back and forth, up and down, with the longe wand. Discuss the significance of removing both halter and lead line. Be sure these items are well away from the fence on the outside.

The instructor or safety support staff person works each new horse first. This is a safety precaution. Check collaborating program's policies and procedures as to whether participants are wearing hard hats during these groundwork sessions. If groundwork with hard hats be sure that staff wear them too. Avoid *'doing as I say not as I do'* mixed messages.

Once all participants have had an opportunity to work their horse in the round ring, give demonstration of the leg up process. Outline the roles of safety side walker, catcher, person giving the leg up, and the horse handler. Mention that the horse handler is almost always a staff person or a knowledgeable, seasoned horse participant with a lot of horse handling experience.

Allow each participant a chance to mount the horse bareback, rotate arms, and swing trunk in brief warm ups at both halt and walk. After a few rounds, have them lean forward, throw leg over horse's back and land on ground walking forward beside the horse. Staff should demonstrate prior to participants doing this exercise. Stress the importance of seeing the picture of the dismount for the horse to read. Some find it easier to talk through the movements aloud.

In the closing circle, begin to discuss differences in learning styles, relational styles, energy styles, communication styles, and how these influence one's experiences. Begin to blend in the learning of the last two days to what might be happening in their home or school environment, with their friends. Work with specific examples. "I notice you work with _____. Is she like anyone else in your life? Or is she more like you? What did you learn that might serve you when making friends, starting a new school year, etc.?"

All staff members make notes in progress log recording the insights being developed by the participants and themselves. How do these relate to their experiences during training week with their own schooling and work with the horses? Designated barn manager keeps work log on the horses, their roles, aptitudes and attitudes, and work history.

DAY THREE: By now, you realize that each session always begins and ends with the circle, mutual choosing, and grooming. The round ring portion may be eliminated unless deemed necessary by instructor to further assist with focus. Horses are tacked with pads, surcingles, bareback pads, headstalls with snaffle bits, and reins have hooks for attachment to the halter.

Students engage in the "rein game", learning to steer each other. Bailing twine is either run through a plastic straw (bit) or laid behind neck and under arms so the person holding the "reins" can steer. Participants form partners. Eliminate adolescent embarrassment of choosing by counting off 1,2,1,2 etc. Designate the 2s to be the six horses. They will then switch roles so both numbers can play as a horse. They can even be a specific horse, perhaps the one they were drawn to during the mutual choosing exercise.

Once paired, go through the schooling lesson of basic walk on, halt, whoa, turns, half turn through the circle, perhaps even trot and or canter. Reverse roles to allow the partners to switch and practice again. This partner lesson in how it feels to have a bit in your mouth, or reins directing your head, is an ideal opportunity to introduce the aids for walk on, halt, turns, and half circles. It also gives the participant an idea of what the horse goes through when having a bit in his mouth. For those who are new to horses, this time provides an opportunity to demonstrate how to hold the reins.

When they are first mounted (using a mounting block and always wearing a hard hat), have them move off and practice the emergency dismount/pony club vault off. Riders are coached to kick their feet free of the stirrups (if worn), lean their bodies forward over the crest of the horse's neck, reins are held in one hand, while the other hand presses on the horse's neck or pommel of the saddle, while flinging one leg over the back of the horse (cantle of the saddle) to land knees bent, walking beside the horse. This practice allows for more mounting and remounting time, practice leading the horse, and offers a real job to the team member(s) waiting their turn in the form of side-walker, and/or safety spotter. It is a good idea to encourage developing proficiency by going to either side of the horse during the emergency dismount/pony club vault off.

Riders practice basic warm up exercises; they are on lead line for the warm-ups with reins attached to the halter. Instructor gives basic skills development lesson, steering, walk halts, two-point position at halt and walk. Allow each team equal time to ride.

Once this initial basic lesson is concluded, have all help put horses and equipment away. Give some grass hay to the horses, if barn manager approves, and circle up for processing. Discuss safety concerns and plan for the next day's work. Again, develop insights with concrete examples of participant's stated experience with your observations and how such learning might serve in their life outside of relational horse skills week/session.

DAY FOUR: Repeat the initial circle, verbal safety agreements, feelings check, centering exercise, energizing and bonding. After the grooming, the horses are tacked, offering participants a choice of equipment. Often participants prefer to stick to the pads, experience real bareback, or ride in a saddle. Ideally there are both Western and English (balanced seat type – avoid saddle seat or extreme close contact jumping saddle) available. For gray area weight issues, a Western saddle distributes the weight more fully on the horse's back. Use high quality cotton or felt pad, or a gel pad. The **AIA** rule is the weight must not hurt the horse and must not hurt the rider.

If saddles are used, only participants wearing boots with a heel may ride in ordinary stirrups. All others (tennis shoes, hiking boots) must have peacocks. Make sure the stirrups are large enough for the toe of the shoe to slip easily out of the stirrup. If in doubt, have them ride without stirrups. It is the best way to acquire a solid independent balanced seat.

Repeat the arena lesson building on basic steering skills, halt and walk. Introduce concept of half halt and practice. Develop and work with basic arena schooling figures. Play follow-the-leader. It may be that you have a student intern or staff member mounted acting as "lead rider". Except in the case of riders with independent seat, the reins remain attached to the halters worn under the headstalls. Practice the rising trot motion while at the walk.

Once everyone has engaged in skills lesson, prepare for short walk on the trail. If time is an issue, have half the group ride out, and the other half ride home. They can either carry their hard hats on the walk, or know the location of the mounted rider wearing the hat they plan to use. Design this walk on the trail to be done in silence. Remember your mission is to facilitate development of relationship(s). Silence on the trail, astride the moving horse, supported by safety spotters and the company of others is a powerful experience. You will discover many of the participants decide voluntarily to close their eyes.

Create hand signals that may be passed from side walker to side walker, or horse handler to horse handler, or safety spotter to safety spotter (depending on skill level) allowing the mounted rider to engage in their own reverie while walking along in nature.

After the horses and equipment are put away, circle up and plan the completion ceremony for last day's work.

DAY FIVE: Completion ceremony is reviewed and discussed in the opening circle. A popular option is Spirit horse painting. In this activity, the participant paints symbols or pictures on the horse with washable tempera paints. Tell the group what the time frame is so they can pace themselves. Make sure to allow time at the end of the painting session for each individual to explain their artwork to the rest of the group. Take a Polaroid picture of participant and their horse for them to take home. This activity requires staff take time for bathing the horses that same day. Weather may be an issue for baths.

Another option is to make horse hoof prints. Lift the horse's hoof, have the participant paint the bottom of the hoof, and then carefully put it down on a plain white piece of heavy card stock paper, creating an imprint. On this paper, write the address as to where the participant can write to their horse during the year. In my belief system, the horses are connected to all with whom they interact, and as in treasured friendships, enjoy catch-up communications.

Other activities may include a short bareback ride on their horses before making the hoof print, or fully tacked horses running relay race games in the arena. Have Fun! KEEP IT SAFE!

HAPPY TRAILS

BKR'S LIST OF FAVORITE READS

Big Book of *Alcoholics Anonymous*
A Course in Miracles
The Black Stallion, Walter Farley
Brighty of the Grand Canyon, Marguerite Henry
Kinship With All Life, J. Allan Boone
Death, Taxes, and Other Illusions, Arnold Patent
Teach Only Love, Jerry Jampolsky, MD
Reinventing Medicine, Larry Dossy, MD
A Cry Unheard, James J. Lynch, MD
The Story of B., Daniel Quinn
Women Who Run With The Wolves, Clarrisa Pinkoles-Estes
Shaman, Healer, Sage, Alberto Vilodo, Ph.D.
Book of Secrets, Deepak Chopra, MD
Positive Energy, Judith Orloff, MD
Animals in Translation, Temple Grandin and Catherine Johnson
The Dog Listener, Jan Fennell
Riding Into The Light, & *Dressage for the 21ˢᵗ Century*, Paul Balisk
Best Horse Video teaching language of Equus:
     Dances With Horses, Carolyn Resnick (760) 743-3377

Anything written by Marion Woodman, Robert Bly, Carl Jung, Stan Grof, Christina Grof, Joseph Campbell, Ayn Rand, Mathew Fox, Barbara Ann Brennan, Caroline Myss, Deepak Chopra, Andrew Weil, Anne Wilson Schaef, Ram Dass, Alice Walker, Martin Luther King, Charles deKnuffy, Sally Swift, Gary Zukav, Fritjof Capra, Mary Wanless, The Dalai Lama and Paul Balisk

Shasta, Archetype of Divine Child in all of us.

HANDBOOK: GLOSSARY

Archetype: representative of predispositions or potentialities for experiencing and responding to the world. These innate behavioral patterns are what Carl Gustav Jung termed archetypes, an original model, and a prototype of a behavioral matrix. Jung said, "Just as instincts compel man to conduct a life that is specifically human, so the archetypes compel intuition and apprehension to form specifically human patterns".

Jung characterized Psyche as an organizing locus for the myth creating level of mind he called the collective unconscious. The collective unconscious is an unlimited reservoir of latent primordial images (archetypes) linking all humanity.

The archetype image represents to consciousness innate predispositions for responding to typical human situations or being in human relationships. Some major archetype images described by Jung are Persona, Shadow, Anima, Animus, Wise Old Man, Great Mother, Miraculous Child, Hero/Savior, Heroine, and Self.

You, dear reader, know by now, I teach with stories. The STIRRUP barn contained within its herd members, representatives of the various archetypical aspects of Psyche. Here from the early days of STIRRUP barn is that of SHASTA (spring, 1992). I quote from my journal about SHASTA:

> The other day, in a budget discussion, a corporate executive invited me to justify "that little hay-burning pony". He was referring to Shasta, our aged (28 years) Palomino Shetland pony mare who only occasionally

pulled a jogging cart. Shasta resembled the classic chubby, "Thewell" pony wearing her blonde fluffy winter coat body clipped with a large heart emblazoned on her rump and the shaggy, shaggy leggings of a mini-Clydesdale.

Shasta came to the STIRRUP Program as a retired therapy pony from a busy program offering services to physically challenged children. She had grown stiff and appeared unable to keep up the work regime. She appeared lethargic and withdrawn. Actually, her attitude and air resembled that of our locked up adolescent youth - depressed. She was in transition and stuck. Was she looking at permanent retirement or was a career re-frame possible?

Our adolescent patients created an individual treatment plan for her remediation, which included much attention and appreciation. The youth focused on designing activities in which they felt she was capable of participating without creating stress or triggering unruly acting out behavior. At the pre-conscious coming into full conscious awareness, these adolescents identified how similar Shasta's presenting symptoms were to their own serious situations.

Loving attention was demonstrated through frequent grooming, long slow walks on the lead line and cross country long reining (ground driving) practice. Most remarkable for all (Shasta, patients, barn and hospital staff), she was given complete freedom in the barn and stable yard.

Complete freedom? Yes! Shasta was allowed to mosey about, or run, or buck, or zip in and out of wherever she pleased. The hay barn was conveniently fenced off. And she did however have an additional "off limits". There is always an "off limits" - even in regular non-institutionalized life. Shasta's was the Field of Dreams; the lush green, irrigated playing field used by the hospital recreational therapy department for its multi-purpose outdoor games. Located adjacent to our STIRRUP Program Barn area, for a loose returning to health and vigor pony, this field's attraction was irresistible.

On rare occasions, unfortunately usually when the aforementioned corporate executive visited, Shasta would forget herself. She would wander over to the tempting lushness of the green grass field. Now, this field had a very expensive underground irrigation system that was not designed to tolerate pony prints. Usually a fairly sharp shout in her direction from the barn staff or an alert patient would send her zipping back to the stable yard at a rapid clip.

Shasta was most frequently seen on a lead line between an adolescent patient and primary counselor who were "walking her out" as part of her remedial conditioning program. Some valuable one on one psychotherapy occurred as patient and counselor joined efforts in helping Shasta with her rehabilitation regimen. Often the patient was most familiar with the appropriate protocol in handling Shasta. The opportunity to establish mutual trust developed as the counselor-patient roles re-framed to patient as teacher and counselor as student engaged in the activity of "walking out" Shasta.

There existed the added element of solidarity as the trio (patient, counselor and pony) were admonished by the horse professional and/or certified instructor to take no "guff" from the maintenance and grounds personnel who were fond of providing jesting remarks centered around the theme of "walking that funny dog". This walk about trio honored the rule of staying within sight and/or shouting distance of barn staff.

Archetypically, Shasta represented that precious perfect core element of us. She embodied love energy. You felt, saw, sensed and knew love with Shasta. She represented our inner perfect precious core of Self where Being is enough.

Spiritually, Shasta anchored our inner knowing integral to healthy function. No activity or achievement required. Our essence recognized and valued. In Shasta's energy field, one felt whole, complete, unique and essential. Shasta represented the healing of our shame; that aspect of our selves that can feel not a part, not necessary to, and not worthwhile. She reminded us our core is love.

Shasta also represented our Inner Child. Present in us all, this Child wants to be given permission to do or to be anything. Her freedom to wander wherever spoke to a need in patients and staff to know that same sense of abundant potential. Her regime of appreciation and affirmation celebrating her being evoked recognition of similar wants within us. We want permission to be bliss, to be passion, to live life in heart.

Shasta's blooming health represented recovery. Her innate gifts and strengths emerged matching those of the adolescent patents. Talents and aptitudes were discovered and flourished. Shasta was the Miraculous Child Archetype.

"This image, often appears in the dreams of a gifted child, is the symbol of new possibility, of growth, of the new attempt, of the joyous renewal of life, of the vision of new beginning. In the negative version, we have such figures as Peter Pan, or the child who never grew up, although always behind such a child image is the possibility of growth and renewal". (Anthony Storr).

Projection: mechanism by which we humans create our experience of reality. The process is known as **transference** and **counter-transference**. A simple version is "I see in you what is actually in me and as this trait, characteristic, behavior, talent or strength is as yet un-integrated and un-known to me I project it out on you as being true of you - having nothing to do with me at all."

Truth is, I am unable to perceive in another person, place or thing, that which is not also present in me.

The next section goes into much more detail about this 'living process'.

CROSS COUNTRY DIALOGUES

You may have heard the news. **Adventures In Awareness** Internship Program (**AIA - IP**) launched in January 2004. This skill based study opportunity working with the **AIA** equine interactive exercises, theory and conceptual framework contains five core courses - 14 days of curriculum.

Optional credit is available through the University of Arizona's Educational Psychology Department at the graduate or undergraduate level. In addition, there are three Enrichment Sections: Equine Skills Development, Equine Facilitated Experiential Learning, and Equine Facilitated Psychotherapy. Further information and specifics of logistics may be found on the **AIA** website: www. adventuresinawareness.net

In responding to a query from Florida, I met and began a discussion with J through e-mail. J identifies as an equine specialist who gives beginner horsemanship and riding lessons while also teaching an equine experiential learning class in collaboration with the community college. She studied the **AIA** website and wrote me to ask about the **AIA** practice of choosing one's own horse.

My response generated more rich questions from J. It occurred to me our **AIA** students may be interested in this cross-country discussion on theory, principle and conceptual framework for equine facilitated experiential learning as viewed through the lens of **Adventures In Awareness.**

Suggesting folks choose a horse is practiced during **AIA** sessions as the "heart scanning" exercise that follows a centering process, preceded by the verbal safety agreement and feelings check in. Within **AIA**'s conceptual framework, this mutual choosing represents the postulate, "we are both students and teachers to each other".

AIA's "heart scanning" exercise is deliberate conscious work with the process of 'projection' defined as seeing in another some element or aspect of myself that I may or may not be conscious or aware also exists in me. The mechanisms of transference and counter transference operate in the projection process ALL THE TIME.

Mystics in the Gnostic traditions say that the process of projection is how concretized reality is formed. "As above so below, as within so without...." Quantum physics and higher mathematics are two sciences proving this truth - reality is projection becoming. Evidence is mounting for there being no "objective reality". Rather, an infinite field of possibilities.

What does this mean for us in equine facilitated experiential learning? How do we take these interpersonal relationship concepts and work with them to benefit our own growth and healing? In ourselves, our participants (students or clients) and our horses?

From my perspective, I see the process of projection as the gate into the round ring of experiential gestalts where we explore these quantum packets of information moment by aware moment. Fueled with heart passion, our conscious or unconscious desire chooses from the Field of Infinite Possibility. Mindful intentional focus co-creates moment by moment our experience. Awareness is the key to beneficial conscious choice.

Yes, it is the process of projection at work when a participant tells you they feel connected to a particular horse and they think this is true because... illustrating with an association or connection to someone they know, or something they are feeling inside. AND THERE IS SO MUCH MORE!

Mutuality of "like attracting like" exists at the level of mental, physical, emotional and spiritual. "Heart scanning" is 'mutual choosing' consciously. There is a zing felt energy "whoosh", an electrical charge between the "heart scanning" human and the particular horse. On the other hand, there may be an absence. A no energy "whoosh" provides information too.

In my worldview, the horses during an **AIA** session also engage in "heart scanning". They have volunteered to co-evolve with the human in moving to another level of awareness in Consciousness. It is this energetic bonding that I hope to study in more depth with some of the emerging telemetry from the world of biofeedback. The Kirlian camera is evolving to where it may soon be possible to photograph these energetic exchanges without total darkness.

As the **AIA** session unfolds, and the heart bond further explored with other equine facilitated interactive exercises, a connection and depth of unfathomable inner world information is frequently revealed. The quality of inner-actions mirrors unknown, unexpressed information of significance to the participant. Over the course of the last 13 years, the remarkable 'unhorseyness' of these exchanges has required me to reframe my notions of human animal trans-species communication.

It is important for human co-facilitator(s) to remain present. They internally scan their own body/mind/spirit for clues generated out of the mechanisms of transference and counter transference. Accepting, allowing, and remaining present are the tasks of the co-facilitators(s) and equine safety support advocate.

I choose the word 'unfathomable' as an accurate descriptor of numinous-ness surfacing to consciousness. The **AIA** participant thus engaged later remarks on a piece of information energetically linking past, present, and future, simultaneously. Pre-cognitive, intuitive and/or remote viewing experiences are not uncommon.

In my experience it is the process of projection consciously embraced, the concurring mechanisms of transference and counter transference reverently acknowledged in attitude of allow, allow, allow – listen, listen, listen – that produces ambience for catharsis and insight. The tradition of psychoanalysis and psychotherapy postulates cathartic emotional release and personally developed insight linked together lay down new neuro pathways in the brain. This re-programming is a particularly empowering experience in the presence of the horse, archetype and mirror for Power, Freedom and Spirit.

PS. J responded by commenting on the postulate of "no such thing as 'objective' reality" and remarked she was glad to not be studying William Glaser's *Reality Therapy*!

My thought, "or Kohut's *Object Relations Theory*".

J then asks, "...about the mechanisms of transference and counter transference? What do these actions/behaviors look like or sound like? How do I know if I, as a facilitator, am transferring or counter transferring?"

From my perspective, we are always transferring and counter transferring. The degree of energetic charge felt by the body as sensations of discomfort signals negative feelings, thoughts, emotions. Felt fully with awareness, we information gather as we allow them to pass on through. The trouble is our culture has taught us to deny, cover up, stuff and suppress our feelings. The warm fuzzy feelings of connection and kinship are the positive side of this energetic charge. It is all energy. Humans label and judge.

Now what about this process of 'judgment'? How does it serve and or hinder us? I am suggesting that when our bright information filled minds are busy evaluating and assessing, we are prey to dangerous miss-perceptions if not consciously centered in our hearts. Ideally, our own inner work has brought us to a mature practiced aware exercise of free will. This ability to choose consciously with awareness, placing our minds in service to our hearts, allows for witness mode and access to truth.

Without the ability to consciously craft this emotional distance one either becomes victim to denial (a form of perceptual blindness) and/or succumbs to taking interactions personally - identifying with 'me' and losing out to the ego personality self's distress. For a specific of how this temptation to fall into diagnostic evaluator mode must be tempered with balance, and the witness active observational mode adopted consciously, I offer this most recent workshop example:

> One of our **AIA** participants was initially distracting, interruptive and confrontational especially to me, the lead facilitator. BR had difficulty with the

safety agreement. She wanted to be responsible for everyone.

"No, confine your concerns to yourself. If you need a break, require a 'time out', have to leave the group for private time, let us know and be willing to take care of yourself."

BR said, "It is easier for me to take care of you. I don't know how to take care of myself".

"Well, this is a safe place to begin practice of self care," I responded. "Remember the safety agreement, *'I am responsible for self today, and thus, contribute to the safety of the group. - Mentally, physically, emotionally, and spiritually'*."

Note: On some level of field reading, I knew that BR did not want to tell the group or me that she smoked. She did not want to acknowledge that smoking was possibly the least of the addictions currently driving her life. Rather, than take her angry outbursts personally, I continued to consciously choose to re-direct and channel this intense energy into the design of our inner active exercises.

Moving through the "heart scanning" exercise and into con su permiso, I suggested all participants begin to develop that simultaneous awareness of feelings flowing through them as they observed each other approach a horse. BR was adamant that a particular horse who had walked up to me, engaged me at the gate of arena, and continued with her 'come hither' invitations for me to scratch a particular area didn't like me.

"She doesn't like you." BR stated flatly.

"Okay, be aware of how that feels in you," I suggested.

"It's not me. She doesn't like you," BR repeated. "I feel fine!"

As others in the group expressed their observations, *"when I see you..., I feel... " it was evident they were experiencing a different reality.*

Rather than evaluate observations as right or wrong, good or bad, the exercise's purpose is to share the rich diversity of our different experiences while observing the same outer action. The source of these observational perceptions originates in the world behind our eyes. *"As above, so below; as within, so without....."*

Carl Jung and Sigmund Freud agreed on few things. One of the principles they did share is that each time I'm attempting to point the finger out there. "She doesn't like you". Three fingers are pointing back at me. "I don't like me".

The purpose of **Adventures In Awareness** Equine Facilitated Experiential Learning process work is to develop awareness of these operating principles and to practice conscious choice of our minds in service to our hearts. Developing abilities to choose behaviors and change feelings with conscious awareness is authentic empowerment.

At lunch, BR revealed more of herself and her story, as we informally fell into girl talk about comfortable shoes. By now, the group had formed a strong heart alliance. Practicing with the teaching story principles of allowing, listening, and trusting the process, group acceptance was melting BR's earlier animosity. She told of her recent class in hands on healing where the teacher had remarked on her strong energy. Telling us about learning to share the heat of her hands to help others made BR's face light up.

Moving to the square round ring, we began our congruent message sending inner active exercise. As the day evolved, many had cathartic experiences.

One participant was not sure she even believed these energetic field readings existed. BB felt a zing of a connection, walked into the arena to ask the question, "What is the teaching?" and had her first horse appear for completion work. BB exited the portal of change acknowledging there is information available and suspension of judgment – just for a nanosecond – will take you there.

When BR honored a particular horse's invitation to share energy, she delighted in the mare's receptivity. Her witnesses offered positive encouragement to continue learning to share her healing hands gift. Then, another horse banged the corral seeking entrance. He wanted BR. Donner was wearing a leather strap around his neck.

"Why does he have that neck collar?" BR asked.

"He's an addict," I responded. "He cannot stop himself from sucking air with his teeth wrapped around the corral post".

"I am an addict." BR flatly stated. She looked up at us, defiance and shyness flashed across her face.

"Well, are not we all in some fashion?" responded BB.

"I go to meetings. I've been to treatment. I just don't seem to be able to stay off the booze or drugs for more than a few months. Then, I'm back at it. I smoke all the time. That's where I've been disappearing to when you take breaks. All you horse people have no smoking policies in your barns. I sneak off. I hate myself for not being able to quit."

"Do you hate Donner?" I ask.

BR is affectionately stroking his mane. "Of course not, he's precious."

"Well, like yourself he struggles with his addiction, cribbing. It is his behavior (wind sucking) that is distressing and endangers his health. Donner, as equine essence is very lovable. Just like you, as human essence are very loveable.

"It is your behavior (drinking, drugging, smoking) that is distressing and endangers your health. Behaviors are subject to change. In this present time as you and Donner share energy, mutually loving each other, neither of you is engaging in addictive behavior."

A huge smile washes over BR's face. She lights up and glows. "That's true and just now, this minute I feel WONDERFUL!"

Donner swings his large head around to cradle her with his neck in the equine mare and foal hug.

"So hold on to this feeling," I counsel. "Allow yourself to be sustained and supported by this feeling. Look out at your support witnesses. Allow us to intentionally support your recovery in Consciousness."

My eyes are awash in tears. Joy, hope, sadness, angst, prayers of sheer gratitude for my own recovery flow through me. Deep inside I breathe into my heart gratitude and deep appreciation for Universal Wisdom.

She so loves a joke. It is not lost on me that this intense projection filled day has given me BR (my own initials) as a mirror.   Compassion for BR and myself floods through me. As BR exits the arena, we hug.

"I get it now. It is me that I didn't like this morning," she says to me.

"And now?" I query.

"Better! Much Better!"

We hug again.

Tucson, AZ 8/04

ABOUT THE AUTHOR

Barbara K. Rector, MA

In 1974, co-founder of TROT (Therapeutic Riding of Tucson, Inc.), Barbara utilized her skills as a Pony Club Instructor to teach - TROT. While acting as Resource Developer, Director of Instruction, and Executive Director, she taught 45 weekly volunteers safe helping and handling techniques, schooled and trained 12 horses and ponies, supervised and developed assistant instructors, while teaching 4 - 6 half day sessions of TROT classes for approximately 80 students a week.

In 1989-90, at The College of the Holy Names in Oakland, CA, she obtained a Master of Arts degree with an emphasis in Spiritual Psychology. While at the Institute of Culture and Creation Centered Spirituality, she worked as an intake counselor and group facilitator for near death youth, and women with homebound disabilities, at the Center for Attitudinal Healing in Tiburon, CA. While completing her thesis, she worked as the manager for NCEFT (National Center for Equine Facilitated Therapy) in Woodside, CA. She is a 1965 graduate of the University of Arizona with a BA in Philosophy and English.

In the early 90s, Barbara developed the therapeutic riding programs at Sierra Tucson and co-founded Flagstaff Equine Therapeutic Enterprises (FETE), in Flagstaff, AZ. At Sierra Tucson, a private psychiatric hospital, she developed and coordinated Sierra Tucson's Integrated Riding Resource Program for adolescents, family week treatment, the eating disorders, and trauma resolution units, while training the hospital medical staff in her model for equine facilitated experiential learning process work – now trademarked as **ADVENTURES IN AWARENESS**™ **(AIA)**.

More recently, Barbara has developed and now directs the **Adventures In Awareness** Internship Program (**AIA** - IP) to provide educators, health, horse, and other animal professionals with an experiential "learning through doing" opportunity to develop competency in the principles, theory, and practice of Equine Facilitated Experiential Learning (EFEL) and Equine Facilitated Psychotherapy (EFP). Students utilize the structure of the **AIA** process to discover their unique gifts and talents while also engaging in a personal growth and development process.

AIA's 5 DAY Equine Experiential Learning Curriculum, an enrichment and prevention program for at risk youth and those with severe emotional and behavioral disturbances features the **AIA** process. This is the core curriculum for many college and university programs offering competency based learning. **AIA** promotes working with horses as a reflection experience, mirroring personal and interpersonal relationships. The specially designed interactive exercises develop communication (including interspecies) skills, promote team building, and contribute to the ability to be responsible for self. Responsible individuals make healthy behavior choices. People who feel empowered live in peace and harmony with self and others.

Barbara has served on the NARHA (North American Riding for the Handicapped) Board of Directors – the Ways and Means and Standards Committees. She co-founded EFMHA (Equine Facilitated Mental Health Association), a section of NARHA, and serves as a board member on the EFMHA Curriculum Development and Standards Committees; as co-chair of EFMHA Standards, she is liaison member to NARHA Standards. She is a founding board member for Animal Therapy Association (ATA) [which merged with People, Animals & Nature (PAN)], an organization developing animal assisted therapy as a profession, linking existing 'model' practices, and generating educational degree programs.

Barbara lives in Tucson where she is OMI to three adorable grandgirls, steward for Cidar and Buttercup and student continuing to learn from the lovely Crone Mare "Ramblin-Kay-Bar (RAMA) now 27 years young. Those seeking further information on where and how to attend **AIA** workshops or become involved in the **Adventures In Awareness** Internship Program may locate further information on the website: www.adenturesinawareness.net

Printed in the United States
70286LV00003B/131

9 781420 853926